Louise E. Shimer Hogan

**History and present status of Instruction in cooking in the
public Schools of New York City**

Louise E. Shimer Hogan

History and present status of Instruction in cooking in the public Schools of New York City

ISBN/EAN: 9783744789059

Printed in Europe, USA, Canada, Australia, Japan

Cover: Foto ©Paul-Georg Meister /pixelio.de

More available books at **www.hansebooks.com**

BULLETIN No. 56.

U. S. DEPARTMENT OF AGRICULTURE,

OFFICE OF EXPERIMENT STATIONS.

HISTORY AND PRESENT STATUS

OF

INSTRUCTION IN COOKING

IN THE

PUBLIC SCHOOLS OF NEW YORK CITY.

REPORTED BY

Mrs. LOUISE E. HOGAN,

WITH AN INTRODUCTION BY

A. C. TRUE, Ph. D.

WASHINGTON:
GOVERNMENT PRINTING OFFICE.
1899.

LETTER OF TRANSMITTAL.

U. S. DEPARTMENT OF AGRICULTURE,
OFFICE OF EXPERIMENT STATIONS,
Washington, D. C., January 25, 1899.

SIR: I have the honor to transmit herewith a report on the history and present status of instruction in cooking in the public schools of New York City, prepared by Mrs. Louise E. Hogan, under the supervision of Prof. W. O. Atwater, special agent in charge of nutrition investigations, in accordance with instructions given by the Director of this Office.

The teaching of cooking as a branch of manual-training courses in the primary and grammar grades of the public schools has been rapidly increasing in favor among school officers and the people in different parts of the country. In connection with the nutrition investigations in charge of this Office numerous inquiries have been received regarding the scope and meaning of such courses and the practicability of their further introduction into the common schools. To meet the evident demand for information on this subject it has been thought desirable to prepare an account of the progress and present development of the teaching of cooking in one of our great educational centers.

In the collection of material for this report substantial aid has been given by Dr. E. D. Shimer, associate superintendent of public schools in New York City, Mrs. M. E. Williams, supervisor of cookery in the New York schools, and other officers and teachers connected with the schools of that city.

The report is transmitted with the recommendation that it be published as Bulletin No. 56 of this Office.

Respectfully,

A. C. TRUE,
Director.

Hon. JAMES WILSON,
Secretary of Agriculture.

CONTENTS.

5

ILLUSTRATIONS.

6

HISTORY AND PRESENT STATUS OF INSTRUCTION IN COOKING IN THE PUBLIC SCHOOLS OF NEW YORK CITY.

INTRODUCTION.

By A. C. True, Ph. D.,

Director, Office of Experiment Stations.

Courses in manual training, including among numerous subjects instruction in cooking, have in recent years been widely introduced into public and private schools of different grades in this country. While at first encountering many objections regarding both their theoretical and practical value, they have steadily increased in favor among school officers and the people who support and patronize the schools. It has been found possible, as regards many of the subjects taught in these courses, so to adjust the relations of the practical exercises to the general educational features as to maintain the interest of pupils in the more routine processes of education, while at the same time furnishing them with some degree of practical skill and knowledge of direct utility to them in the various industries on which the livelihood of the masses of our population depend.

Another effect of manual training, which has already been observed and which will increase in importance as such instruction is more widely diffused, is largely to divest the common industries of those elements of drudgery which tend to make them very distasteful to our more intelligent youth. When the operations of the household, the farm, and the shop are shown to call for trained skill and scientific knowledge in order that they may be most easily and efficiently performed, it becomes apparent that these vocations, as well as the so-called professions, offer abundant opportunities for the exercise of educated brains. Life in these industries is no longer a dull round of routine without beauty or the hope of better things. "I am going to an agricultural college," said a farm boy this summer, "because I believe that what I shall learn there will enable me to get more out of my land and give me more interest and pleasure in my daily work on the farm."

It is true that such courses are of so comparatively recent introduction into our schools that they are far from perfect in many of their details and the opinions of experts are widely at variance on many ques-

7

tions affecting the exact extent and scope of industrial education. The general usefulness of such education is, however, thoroughly established and much has been accomplished in working out its adjustment to the other departments of our educational system.

The teaching of cooking and other subjects connected with domestic science and practice in our colleges, especially those receiving appropriations from the National Treasury under the Morrill Act, special cooking schools, principally under private auspices in our large cities, and courses in cooking for young pupils in private and public schools in many localities have attracted a rapidly increasing number of students and engaged the services of competent and enthusiastic teachers. Begun in a comparatively simple and practical way, these courses have steadily demanded more elaborate equipment, more systematic and thorough instruction, and a larger basis of scientific and pedagogical principles and facts.

Fortunately, the time has also been ripe for the rapid development of original investigations at home and abroad along the lines of chemical and biological studies relating to the food and nutrition of man. Among the agencies which have enjoyed relatively ample means for the prosecution of scientific inquiries in this direction have been the Division of Chemistry and the Office of Experiment Stations of this Department. Much of this work has been done in cooperation with colleges, experiment stations, "social settlements," and other organizations in different parts of the country. The investigations pursued by other Divisions of the Department have also contributed considerable information of value to students in domestic science. Special efforts have been made to acquaint officers and teachers of schools of different grades with the results of this work and the publications of the Department are now widely used in connection with such courses of instruction. The accumulating mass of accurate data in this line of scientific inquiry has enabled teachers to systematize and strengthen their lessons on foods and cooking, as well as on the general principles of nutrition. It has also shown the necessity of more thorough training of teachers of domestic science in order that their instruction may be based on definite knowledge and that they may be able to distinguish between what is mere theory or matter of opinion and what is actually ascertained fact.

As interest in the teaching of topics relating to the food and nutrition of man has grown in this country this Department has been more frequently called upon to furnish information regarding the scope and purpose of such courses and the practicability of their further introduction into our common schools. To meet this growing demand it has been thought desirable to collate and publish an account of the progress and present development of the teaching of cookery in one of our great educational centers. It is believed that this report will also be of service in showing the defects, as well as the excellencies, of such courses as are ordinarily given in our schools. It will constitute material for the further discussion of the principles and details of such instruction with reference to their perfection. It should, therefore, be understood that the course and sample lessons herewith presented are not given because they are believed to show a system which should be followed in all its details, but rather because they are exponents of a successful attempt to introduce the teaching of cooking into the common schools of a large city, and indicate a serious purpose on the part of officers and teachers managing this course to adapt it to the actual requirements of their schools and to change and improve it from time to time as added experience shows ways in which it may be improved.

Another object in issuing this report is to show to those who are vitally interested in the progress of the common schools in country districts, because they themselves are residents of our rural communities, something of the organized effort which is being made to adapt the courses of instruction in our city schools to the actual needs of the youth as they go out into the real work of life. A great revolution is going on in our educational system in the towns and cities. In a number of different directions opportunities are being offered the pupils in our public schools in the larger communities to prepare themselves directly for the different industries of the home, the shop, and the factory. This movement has as yet hardly reached our rural schools, and very many school officers in our smaller communities are not aware of the progress which has been made in this direction in the towns. It is believed, therefore, that a report on the teaching of cookery in New York City is well worthy the attention of people living on farms and in villages. If it is a good thing to have the girls of New York City taught better methods of cooking and the reasons why good housekeeping is vitally connected with the health and general welfare of our people, surely it must be equally desirable that up-to-date information on such subjects should be imparted in our country schools. It is true there are great difficulties to be overcome before such instruction can be efficiently given in sparsely settled regions, but if once the principle is established in the public mind that such instruction should be an essential part of a common school course, without doubt ways and means will be devised for its general dissemination.

REPORT ON COOKING IN THE PUBLIC SCHOOLS OF NEW YORK CITY.

By Louise E. Hogan.

There is a growing interest in the subject of the food and nutrition of man throughout the country. Our people are awakening to the importance of the practical application of scientific research in this direction, and the question naturally arises, What place should this work take in the schools and to what extent can it be introduced? The history of the movement that brought the teaching of cooking into the public schools of New York City may serve to show the pedagogical as well as the practical value of this branch of manual training. The object of presenting such a history is naturally constructive and is intended to arouse further interest in this important educational movement, to show its usefulness by the results already attained, and also to suggest methods for its further extension.

In 1887 the board of education of New York City, after a very careful inquiry into the subject of manual training, concluded that it might be well to incorporate this work into the public school system and the committee in charge stated it to be their opinion that the introduction of what is generally known as manual training would be an improvement in the course of study.

In consequence the board caused to be prepared a course in manual training which began at the lowest primary grade and progressed through every succeeding grade of the primary and grammar school grades. This course was placed under the immediate control of the committee on the course of study which was given authority to determine what modifications, if any, should be made in the course, and what schools should be permitted to introduce it upon application of the boards of school trustees. The first school to adopt the new course entered upon it February 1, 1888, and by the end of December, 1890, no less than 19,476 pupils were pursuing the regular manual training course of study.

Commissioner Holt when presenting to the board the first report of the committee on the course of study in regard to manual training said:

The committee on the course of study, to which was referred the subject of the introduction of manual training into our common schools, respectfully report that they have given to the matter the careful, deliberate, and extensive consideration and investigation which its importance demands.

Inquiry into its origin and development in Russia, Germany, France, England, and other foreign countries shows that its leading purpose in Europe is to foster industrial skill and to produce specialists—artisans—in order to advance the interests which

10

these manufacturing nations have in domestic and foreign trade. Only incidental reference is had in most cases to its general educational, disciplinary, and intellectual relations.

It also appears that the department of education now generally known as manual training was introduced into this country by certain broad-minded, practical educators, to whom its educational possibilities presented themselves as its chief claim for adoption.

Under the lead and example of the educators referred to, much of the detail of the plans and purposes of the European system has been judiciously modified, and the subject made more fit to be incorporated into our system of popular instruction.

It has long been a matter of deep regret and even of apprehension that a large proportion of our young people are growing up with a positive distaste for manual labor. With an ever-increasing number almost any other form of occupation is preferred.

The introduction of manual training in some one or more of its various forms into many of the schools of higher educational institutions of the country has already begun to exert an influence toward bringing about a better state of things. It can not be doubted that this result must become more and more manifest when this training in suitably modified forms becomes the common possession of schools and pupils of every grade.

After consideration of the facts and arguments presented your committee has come to the following conclusions:

(1) That the introduction of what is generally known as manual training would be an improvement to our present course of study.

(2) That manual training is admissible into our schools only as a means of general, and not of special, education.

(3) That, notwithstanding the misdirection of some of the efforts heretofore made in manual training, there are certain manual operations which time and experience have sufficiently tested to demonstrate their usefulness and their availability.

These operations have the following characteristics: They are such as to lead the pupil to acquire correct conceptions of form through the careful and systematic discipline of his sense perceptions and to require as a test of the accuracy of these conceptions their correct manual embodiment in material, and further, to give a practical knowledge of natural laws and of the qualities of materials.

They are within the scope of the faculties of all children whose minds and bodies are in a normal condition. Their results are of general, if not universal, utility as personal acquirements, apart from the educational value of the process. They are comparatively inexpensive, and their introduction will require but little room. They can be taught with but moderate addition to our present force of teachers. For such instruction the following, which are not included in our present course of study, seem eminently suitable, viz, carpenter work, modeling in clay, construction work, drawing to scale, sewing, cooking.

By judicious modification and extension the well-established methods of the kindergarten may readily be made available for the primary and lowest grammar school grades, so as to form with the subject already suggested a complete and continuous course.

(4) That training in these branches, if adopted, should not be for a few selected hundreds of school children, but should be made an essential part of the authorized course of study for all.

(5) That the regularity and continuity of school work should not be interrupted by sending out pupils for instruction elsewhere than in the school building to which they belong.

(6) That the length of the school session should not be extended beyond the present limit.

(7) That provision must be made for suspending the introduction of some of the proposed work in certain schools. The carpenter work and the cooking will require

the setting apart of a room for each purpose. This in some schools it would be impossible to do at once. It would probably not be possible in the first year to introduce the kitchen and workshop into more than one-third of the grammar-school departments.

During their deliberations the committee adopted resolutions for the establishment of this work, one of which reads as follows:

Resolved, That in the girls' grammar schools cooking should be taught in the third and second grades.[1] That instruction in cooking and shop work should be suspended as to each school until a suitable room is provided through the action of the trustees. That the instruction in shop work, cooking, and sewing should be under the direction of special teachers, who should be licensed, employed, and paid in the manner now provided for special teachers. That to secure efficient instruction an additional assistant superintendent should be appointed whose special duty should be to supervise under the city superintendent all the work in manual training in the primary and grammar schools.

The estimated expense of introducing the kitchen outfits was $200 per department, 60 departments, $12,000; kitchen supplies, $100 per department, 60 departments, $6,000. The estimated expense of maintaining the kitchen outfit in succeeding years was $1,200, and for kitchen supplies $6,000. In this report mention is made of two schools in New York City in which cooking was already taught. One of them was the Wilson Industrial School for Girls, in which school the pupils were under 12 years of age, and who after leaving generally became self-supporting. The teachers of this school stated that the kind of instruction given waked the children up mentally, and was favorable for fitting them for the duties of active life. In another school, at No. 9 University Place, New York, an industrial institution under Miss Alice Burns, consisting of several classes which met at different times, there was an excellently equipped cooking room for a class of sixty.

Going into practical operation in the year 1888, manual training gradually commended itself to teachers and trustees until it nearly reached the limit prescribed by the board as proper, in view of the necessity for what may be called conservative progress in the experimental stage of a new and important departure.

The report on this work made by City Superintendent John Jasper for the first year after its introduction is as follows:

This highly interesting method of instruction has been pursued in twenty schools and departments during the last year. * * * The total numer of pupils in these schools and departments is about ten thousand, and steadily, carefully, and encouragingly have these children worked in the course mapped out by the board of education. Owing to the shortness of the period during which the experiment has been tried, it would be unwise to express a definite opinion in regard to the future of manual training. From present appearances, however, it is certain that the children have a love for it, and the parents have a keen appreciation of its advantages. The progress that has been made in the initial stage of a new and untried method is to be highly commended, and the readiness with which most of the teachers have fallen into line in the effort to help the good work along is greatly

[1] At this time there were in the primary schools 6 and in the grammar schools 8 grades, the first being the highest.

to their credit. They aim at opening channels for the development of manly and womanly qualities, hitherto more or less unobserved or unpopular, that must and will have a powerful bearing on the future happiness and prospects of the nation. All the branches of this course of study are thriving—and there is an important point—all the branches, separation of them being impossible. People who dream of pedagogic branches and of manual-training branches in the same department as separate and unrelated things have not yet grasped the subject. The manual of this course of study has been arranged so that all the branches of education are interwoven in such a manner as to make a distinction impossible. It does not mean merely the training of the hand; it means the training of our every faculty. The fundamental truths underlying the manual training methods should, above all things, be known and understood by the teachers and public generally. They aim at no specialty of any kind—no carpentry, no art in designing or modeling, cooking, or sewing, no geometry or mechanical drawing as such—they simply aim at a rational means to obtain and transmit useful knowledge.

In this report for 1888 mention is made of the employment of two special cooking teachers under the manual-training course—one at $1,200 and one at $600—and the equipment of kitchens in five grammar schools at an expense of $3,392.09. A further note is made of an expenditure of $68 for kitchen supplies.

The committee in charge of this work states that it has reason to believe that further application will be made for the full manual-training course when the necessary accommodations can be found, and there should, therefore, be provision made for a moderate increase in the number of manual-training schools; that to maintain the manual-training course during the year 1889 in the schools where it is now in operation there will be required, approximately, $10,000, and it is recommended that this amount be increased in the annual estimate to $25,000, so as to provide for an increase in the number of such schools.

The principal of one grammar school reports that she has observed upon the part of her pupils increased mental activity and a greater interest in all their studies. She says further:

As to its moral aspect, I find it an educational element of much value. It inculcates the dignity of labor, cultivates habits of industry, and opens to girls new avenues for self-support. Parents of the pupils express themselves heartily in favor of the new course, and the results generally are so favorable that your committee may feel somewhat repaid for the great labor and expense incurred by them.

Elizabeth Cavannah, the principal of another grammar school, reports:

The cooking has been enthusiastically received by the pupils and never have I seen more thoroughly interested workers than there are in that branch of the course. Many report from week to week the results of home work, thus giving proof of the hold it has upon them, and parents are constantly signifying their gratification at its introduction.

The study of the chemistry of cooking and an intelligent application of this knowledge can not fail to work a complete revolution in the homes of thousands who now suffer from ignorance of the simplest laws governing the proper preparation of food.

Its educational advantage is manifested in the gradual development of self-reliance and judgment in pupils who are particularly weak in these respects, and in corresponding improvement in those who are naturally stronger.

W. H. J. Sieberg, the principal of a third grammar school, reports:

There has been no deterioration in the effectiveness of study in the pedagogic branches. The children have entered with a will and with zest into the manual-training branches, and the results have been a pleasurable surprise to them, their teachers, and myself. Shop work and kitchen have been aids to discipline.

Another principal reports:

My experience thus far in industrial education in our schools leads me to conclude that the course of instruction in sewing and cooking is beneficial to the pupils of our school, inasmuch as the systematic and philosophic methods laid down for both of these departments must necessarily result in inoculating habits of attention, neatness, and judgment which will benefit children not only in these special branches but in all others during school life, and which will prove of inestimable value in after life.

The following notes on the manual-training course of study appear in the annual report of the board of education following the one quoted from above:

This highly interesting course has proved very successful, not only in the spread of the schools, but also in the satisfactory manner in which it has been carried on. One year ago the whole matter was tentative and many expressed grave doubts as to the feasibility; to-day it has been made in modified form the basis of the general course of study to be pursued by the schools in the city.

The cooking school course, as outlined in the report for 1889, is as follows:

Cooking.—Materials of the human body; waste and repair of tissues.
Digestibility.—Cooking solid materials to prepare them for digestion.
Nutritiveness.—Nutritive values of food; palatability.
Food elements.—Mineral; starch and sugar; fats; albuminoids.
Related facts.—Physical effects of heat on albumen: on starch; on gluten, etc.; proper temperatures for various purposes; chemical effects of overheating and of yeast; important function of the sugar in flour.
Utensils.—Their selection, use, and preservation.
Purchasing food.—Discrimination as to wholesome and unwholesome; choice of parts.
The "germ theory."—Applied to foods.
Practical exercises in cooking.—These involve simple applications of facts and principles taught.

In 1889, at the twenty-seventh annual convocation of the University of the State of New York, held July 9 to 11, an address on the possibilities and limitations of manual training in the public schools of New York City was presented by Prof. Edgar D. Shimer, then professor of philosophy at the New York City University and now associate superintendent of public schools for the borough of Manhattan and the Bronx, New York City. In this address Dr. Shimer first defines manual training as it was then accepted by the New York school authorities before outlining the possibilities and showing the limitations.

In his report he alludes to the want of skilled teaching in manual training, and says this points toward the restoration of the old Saturday normal schools or some other means for the further training of teachers. He speaks of the voluntary conferences among the teachers after school as furnishing supplementary aid to individual effort. He says:

Superintendent Jasper continues fixed in his determination not to approve a course of manual training adapted to a select few with special aptitude, or a course in which any of the branches are taught chiefly as ends in themselves. If it is good for the few to develop and round out their lives, he claims that it is good for the many; if cooking is to be taught merely as cooking, he is opposed to it; but if instruction in the philosophy of cooking, the chemistry of food, and its hygienic application is such as to make more thoughtful and intelligent pupils, the dishes being mere incidents, he favors it. It is on this broad sense of manual training that the work in the New York public schools is based, and the distinct claim is put forth that New York City is the first city in the United States that has made general manual training a part of the regular course.

The main reflex advantage of this movement is that the people are inclined to keep their children at school longer, because the children themselves are more inclined to stay.

If manual training were admissible on no higher ground than this, it would be a proper expedient to serve as a magnet for holding the child while his development proceeds on those lines of the curriculum which are acknowledged by all to lead to mental and moral power.

Whatever interpretation or restriction others may put upon the term, it is plain that in New York public schools manual training is taken to be the development of mind in the training of thought acquisition and thought expression by other than merely verbal means—by operations performed with the aid of the hands, by the manipulations of materials, by appealing to the sense of touch and to muscular sensibility, or the sixth sense, as well as to the senses of sight and sound. Indeed, wise provisions have been made for the training even of the lowest senses of smell and taste, so that on the whole the manual-training idea comprehensively viewed is a more complete scientific and systematic sense training than has been in vogue; a fuller presentation to the mind of sensations, the simple factors or elements of mental life, out of which by the elaborative powers of the conscious self the complicated phenomena of a higher mental life are evolved.

Dr. Shimer says further:

It would be a work of supererogation to enter upon any argument to show, by a priori principles, why the facts reported by the practical workers in manual training in New York City should be just what they are. Expression of thought in any form gives the best assurance of its acquisition. This working principle has been acted on under all theories of education time out of mind. In measuring, matching, marking, the child is not only systematically furnished with a store of concepts through its primary perceptions, but these are at the same time riveted. The work furnishes, too, an admirable outlet for the surplus store of nervous energy found in childhood. It exercises, why should it not therefore develop, the attention, judgment, and especially the will? It calls for exactness and promotes habits of persistence, industry, fidelity, thoroughness, honesty, and self-reliance.

Whatever may be said of the indirect results of physical culture, respect for manual labor, and handiness for the emergencies of daily life, the benefits of manual training in the New York public schools are not conceived to be social or economic or utilitarian.

The possibilities, both theoretical and practical, point in a different direction, as I have tried to show. Some of these possibilities have become certainties under the very eyes of expert teachers, whose judgment was held in abeyance until they had exchanged theories for facts. Such limitations as are extrinsic to the subject largely depend for their removal upon the activity of the committee of the board of education.

Such other limitations as appear to be intrinsic, but really lie in a misconception of the end in view, or of the means to be applied, will be removed by the progressive training of the teachers, for in this, and in this almost alone, lies every educational hope for the future.

The experiment was looked upon as successful a year ago. It is no longer an experiment. In every case expectations have been more than realized, and there is no doubt that manual training has come into New York City public schools to stay.

Principal F. S. Capen, of the New Paltz Normal School, in his remarks on this report said:

A wrong opinion prevails with reference to the subject, and this is the reason why it meets with so much opposition. I heard a paper and discussion in the State association at Brooklyn, and the subject met there with very much opposition. It meets with opposition oftener, perhaps, than it meets with favor. When I have been asked whether I favor it or not, I have always so far said I do not know. But I am prepared to say here, in the light of the paper just read, that if that is manual training I am in favor of it. The opinion prevails largely with teachers, and still more largely with those who send their children to our schools, that manual training means the learning of a trade, that it means making mechanics, cooks, seamstresses, etc. That, of course, we can not do in the schools, and it is a mistake to undertake it. Just as much a mistake to undertake to do that as it is to make a theologian, or a lawyer, or a teacher in a college. It can not be done and do thorough work. If manual training is to be used to make men and women more competent to whatever they undertake to do in life, then we can use it.

In the annual report to the board of education for 1890 the number of schools and departments pursuing the manual-training course of study is stated to be 37, and the whole number of pupils registered in this course is 19,904, with an average attendance of 19,482. The schools consist of male grammar departments 7, female grammar departments 8, mixed grammar departments 1, primary departments 13, and primary schools 8.

There were 185 classes in sewing, containing 5,720 pupils; 26 classes in cooking, containing 891 pupils; and 52 classes in workshop (wood working), containing 1,690 pupils.

All the pupils received instruction in the English branches and in drawing (free-hand and mechanical), and modeling in clay was carried on from the lowest primary through five of the eight grammar grades.

The course pursued in this class of schools seemed to be meeting with general approval, and the instruction was efficient.

The report states that—

It was not the purpose to make of the pupils either artists or artisans, seamstresses or cooks, but it was the purpose of the framers of the new plan to determine definitely whether the manual-training appliances and methods would prove as effective educational agents and forces as appeared probable.

The course of study was prepared from a strictly educational point of view, for it was generally agreed that nothing in the laws of this State authorized the diversion of the common-school funds to the purposes of industrial education or the teaching of special trades. A few of the fundamental principles involved, as

17

given in a circular of information by the United States Bureau of Education in 1881, may shed some light on this aspect of the subject:

"(1) The State has a right to teach any branch of knowledge that will promote the public welfare.

"(2) The right of the State to teach all knowledge does not necessarily make such instruction its duty. The right to teach is one thing and the obligation to teach is another. The duty of the State in education is limited by its ability.

"(3) The duty of the State to teach is also conditioned by necessity.

"(4) The primary and imperative duty of the public school is to provide training and to teach knowledge of general application and utility. The primary function of the public school is of the highest practical importance and value. Its comprehensive aim is to prepare the child to discharge the duties and meet the obligations of coming manhood, including his relations to the family, society, and the State, relations involving the highest and most important activities of civilized life.

"(5) The public school, as above defined, exhausts neither the right nor the duty of the State in education. The State may establish higher institutions, and it may organize and encourage special schools to promote important industries or to meet the wants of classes. It has the right to supplement the public school by special schools for technical training. * * * The elements of technical knowledge which are of general application and utility may clearly be taught in the public schools. * * * Such instruction is not only the basis of technical training, but it is of great value to all youth, whatever may be their future occupations and positions in life. It is useful as a preparation for all pursuits. * * * Time for this instruction may be gained by reducing the time hitherto devoted to several other branches of study. This has been done in many schools without loss, and the adoption of truer ideas and better methods of teaching would make it possible and feasible to all. * * * Such instruction may properly be called general, in distinction from that which relates to a particular trade or pursuit, which is special."

The objection to special technical training does not apply to the training of pupils in the use of hand tools and simple mechanical processes, when such training is made a means of general education, the training of the eye, the hand, the mind, for educational purposes. Such training is not the teaching of trades or handicraft, but is general technical training, the same as mechanical drawing, and as such has a place in the public-school course.

The extent of such training will depend upon its value as an element of general education. The public school can not easily undertake the work of special technical training. * * * The public school has done its part in preparing youth for special pursuits when it has given them an efficient general preparation for all pursuits, and all industrial experience shows that the more fundamental and thorough this general preparation, the more fruitful will be the special training.

In the report to the board of education for 1891, under the heading of "Course of study," it is stated that—

No modification has been made during the year, and there are 37 departments pursuing the manual-training course of study, 122 classes in sewing, 22 in cooking, and 55 in workshop. The course pursued in this class of schools seems to be meeting general approval and the instruction is efficient.

In December of the same year a special report was made on this subject, and some improvements were made as suggested by experience. The comment on cooking is as follows:

This subject is taught to the girls in the second and third grammar grades. The teaching is done by four special teachers. The progress made has been commendable, the instruction having been given in thorough accord with the specifications

9900—No. 56——2

of the course of study. The real object of the study has been kept carefully in view, and the understanding of food values, chemical changes, hygienic influences, and physiological truths has not been sacrificed for the simple ability to make palatable dishes. The choice of raw materials, their composition, their nutritive quality, and their relative values have been carefully studied, and the change of food into blood is understood from an economical as well as a scientific point of view.

A note is also made on the influence of the manual-training course as follows:

The question of the amount and character of the influence which the so-called manual-training subjects exert upon the ordinary branches of school education is one that is not to be settled by mere offhand statement. The correct answer can not be given by the enthusiast, who finds in manual training a panacea for all the ills of school life, and who sees in the shop work or in the cooking an ennobling influence that transforms the character of the wayward pupil; nor can it be given by the half-hearted, doubting teacher who fails to give to the pupils a fair opportunity to obtain the benefit to be obtained from the really excellent methods which are characteristic of the manual-training course.

The true condition of affairs can be determined only by carefully and dispassionately viewing the whole field, and by obtaining, as nearly as may be done, the consensus of judgment of those who have been responsible for the application and enforcement of the provisions of the manual-training course of study. Probably the true condition of the situation is this: The manual-training subjects lead the pupil to see and to understand more things, and consequently give them more subjects to talk about understandingly and compel them to talk more.

The report of 1892 shows 594 pupils receiving instruction in cooking.

In the same year's report of free lectures given to working men and women, many of whom were the parents of the children attending school, six were said to be on physiology and hygiene and one on the digestion of food. Another interesting note during this year is that it appears to be a fact that the teachers and the pupils who do the best work in manual-training departments are those who do the best work in their regular studies. It is stated that the instruction continues to be of a very satisfactory character, and that the introduction of the manual-training course of study into other schools, as opportunity may offer, would seem to be advisable. It is also urged that the kitchens should be provided with food cabinets and with simple chemical appliances for demonstrating the changes that take place in converting raw material into food and food into blood.

The report of 1893 states that the number of manual-training schools has not been increased, but that this has happened through want of necessary funds and not through lack of desire to introduce the manual-training course into other schools.

The working of the full manual-training course of study in our schools has been very successful. The schools of this class have been visited by many educational experts and by residents of their respective localities. The commendations of these visitors have been, as a rule, of the strongest possible character, and they indorse most fully the New York theory that manual training is not something for the kindergarten and high school simply, but is an educational principle that should permeate the whole course of instruction.

It may be noted in passing that within this year the committee of fifteen of the National Educational Association reports as follows:

Sewing and cooking have the same (but stronger) claims for place in schools as the use of tools of wood and iron. One-half day in each week for one-half a year each in the seventh and eighth grades will suffice for manual training, the sewing and the cooking being studied by the girls and the wood and iron work by the boys.

During 1894 the manual-training course of study was followed without any modification, and there was but slight change in the number and organization of the schools pursuing this course of study.

It was then believed that when all the promotions to the grammar department of the manual-training school would come from primaries in which sewing is thoroughly taught it would be possible to complete the course in sewing by the end of the fifth grade, thus giving more time, if desired, to the subject of cooking and making it feasible to introduce a short course in the chemistry of foods.

In the year 1895 this course of study was established in two more schools. A careful supervision of the instruction in cooking showed thorough and appreciative work. In a few cases the results were attained under difficulties. It should be borne in mind that the appliances necessary for this work had then been in use for some time, and in several schools they needed to be renewed. The course then embraced instruction in the chemistry of foods, and this received its proper share of attention. The practical work was so arranged that each pupil shared in the actual process of cooking the materials selected, under the direct and close supervision of the teacher. Pupils often brought articles cooked by them at home, and the results of the instructions were thus readily seen by the teachers.

In this report there was a note made of the fact that there should be in each school where this subject is taught a collection of charts showing the various cuts of meats and samples of the various kinds of food products.

During the year 1896 the manual-training course was established in two more schools and a supervisor of manual-training subjects was appointed for the first time, the office of supervisor having been created by the board of education under authority vested in it by the new school law.

The teaching of cooking, like other specialties, was provided with a supervisor, the appointment being made in the latter part of October. In the short time intervening between the date of appointment and the close of the year the supervisor held a conference with the special teachers of cooking at which suggestions were made as to the methods of instruction, and these suggestions were supplemented by special advice given at the time of the visits to the several schools. More attention to the chemistry of foods was urged and the introduction of the systematic use of the microscope was recommended.

The plan of work arranged by the supervisor of cookery appointed at this time for the New York schools was as follows:

I. SUBJECTS.—Chemistry, physics, botany, physiology, and hygiene, and their application.

II. WORK.—Work should be made uniform throughout schools as far as possible.

    (1) *Uniformity of science and principles.*—Although science and principles should be the same throughout, dishes may vary according to needs of special schools.

    (2) *Uniformity of time.*—A time-table should be submitted.

III. MEETINGS.—Meetings of teachers should be called at regular intervals.

    (1) *Books.*—Suggestions as to books, apparatus, chemicals, to be used.

    (2) *Methods.*—Methods of presenting different subjects and manner of serving dishes should be discussed.

    (3) *Reading of papers.*—Papers should be read by teachers on special subjects.

    (4) *Assistance to teachers.*—To guide teachers in fitting themselves to teach the different subjects.

IV. ACQUAINTANCE WITH WORK.

    (1) *Classes.*—To visit classes regularly. Suggestions made and help given to teachers. Examine reports of work done by pupils at home and in school.

    (2) *Schools.*—Different schools visited with view of introducing subjects.

    (3) *Institutions.*—Visit Wesleyan University and other institutions for benefit of system.

V. EXAMINATIONS.—To assist in examination of applicants when requested.

VI. REPORTS.—To supply reports as committee may desire.

The order of the cooking lessons in the third and second grades at this date, with suggestions for practical work, is of interest.

ORDER OF COOKING LESSONS.

THIRD GRADE.

Elements in the body and in food. How food repairs the body; why necessary to be repaired. Combustion; oxygen necessary to support combustion both in the body and in the stove. The making and care of a fire.

Boiling—the conversion of water into steam; temperatures of boiling, simmering, and scalding water.

Boiled eggs; coagulation of albumen shown by use of test tube. The composition of egg; how to know a fresh one; how to keep, etc. Poached eggs.

Boiled potatoes; baked potatoes; composition of potatoes; classes of vegetables; potato a tuber; manner of planting; how to keep, etc. Show how starch is extracted.

Boiled rice; steamed rice; the different cereals; composition of rice; its growth; preparation for market, etc. Oatmeal, composition of grain; nutritive value compared with that of rice.

Baked apples; composition of apple, etc.

Bread: Composition of flour; wheat an important cereal; contains more gluten. Show how gluten is extracted from flour.

Omelet.

Milk toast.

Muffins.

Coffee: The coffee berry; the seeds roasted to develop flavor; caffeine; tannic acid; the effect of each.

Meat: Different kinds; the effect of cold and hot water upon meat; different ways of cooking meat in water; composition of beef.

Beef tea: Illustrating the principle of soup making.

Broiling.

Biscuit.

Tea: The tea plant; how prepared; theine similar to caffeine; tannic acid, etc.

Fried potatoes: Principles of frying; temperature of fat, etc.

Corn bread: Composition of corn meal; nutritive value compared with other cereals; different preparation from corn. -

Scrambled eggs.

Soup stock: Soups with stock and soups without stock.

Tomato soup without stock: Should not be cooked in tin vessels, as tomatoes contain much acid.

Baked macaroni with cheese: What macaroni is and how prepared; cheese from the caseine of milk.

Beef stew: Principles of stewing; portions of meat which may be used.

Plain rice pudding.

Steamed brown bread: Principles of steaming.

SECOND GRADE.

Creamed eggs.

Baked custard.

Roast beef: Different cuts roast, etc.

Browned potatoes.

Cocoa: The cocoa bean obtained from the cocoa tree; chocolate and cocoa prepared from same bean.

Breaded chops.

Apple cake with lemon sauce.

Fish balls; why salting preserves food, etc.

Gingerbread.

Chicken: How to tell a young one; how to prepare for roasting; trussing, etc.; how to carve.

Molasses gems.

Plain cake.

Boiled custard.

Pea soup: Composition of peas; value as a food.

Cookies.

Oyster soup.

Cottage pudding.

Boiled fish: Egg sauce—different kinds; how to tell fresh fish, etc.

Creamed potatoes.

Bread pudding.

Griddle cakes.

Meat balls.

Pastry.

Lobster: How to tell a good one, etc.

COOKING FOR INVALIDS.

Mutton broth with rice.

Clam broth.

Chicken broth.

Beef tea.

Farina gruel.

Irish-moss lemonade.

Flaxseed lemonade.

Lemon jelly.

Jelly water.

Toast water.

Chemistry lessons according to manual.

Composition on the chemistry of foods once every four weeks.

SUGGESTIONS FOR PRACTICAL WORK.

The making and care of a fire.

Hard-boiled eggs.

Soft-cooked eggs.

Poached eggs on toast.

Beef tea.

Boiled beef.

Boiled potatoes.

Baked potatoes.

Extraction of starch from potatoes.

The making of a stew.

Steamed rice.

Boiled rice.

Soup stock.

Broiled steak.

Broiled chops.

A lesson on waste meats.

A lesson on frying.

Boiling oatmeal and other cereals.

Wheat muffins.

Baked apples.

Making of coffee.

Plain omelet.

Tea.

Tomato soup with rice.

Tea biscuit.

Lessons on bread making, extraction of gluten from flour.

Cocoa.

Pea soup with croutons.

Baked custard.

Corn muffins.

Plain rice pudding.

Cottage pudding with lemon sauce.

Milk toast.

SUGGESTIONS FOR PRACTICAL WORK—Continued.

Codfish balls.
Gingerbread.
Mashed potatoes.
Popovers.
Steamed brown bread.
Oyster soup.
Molasses gems.
Creamed potatoes.
Baked fish.
Scrambled eggs.
Potato soup.
Chocolate.
Creamed codfish.
Griddle cakes.
Preparing a chicken to roast.
Mock bisque soup.
Plain cake, with suggestions for fancy cake.
Clam soup.

Junket made with pepsin.
Boiled fish with egg sauce.
Macaroni with tomato sauce.
Whole-wheat gems.
Potato salad.
Corn-starch blancmange.
Queen of pudding made with bread crumbs.
Omelet souffle.
Pastry, with suggestions for different kinds of pies.
Dutch apple cake with sauce.
Graham pudding.
Jumbles.
Sponge cake.
Lemon jelly.
Tapioca cream.
Snow pudding with boiled custard.

SPECIAL FOODS FOR INVALIDS.

Beef tea made in a bottle.
Mutton broth with boiled rice.
Crust coffee.
Indian-meal gruel
Barley gruel.
Oatmeal gruel.

Irish-moss lemonade.
Irish-moss blancmange.
Flour souffle.
Stewed oysters.
Brown-bread brewis.

The following are samples of the reports made to the city superintendent of schools regarding the courses in cooking in each school during this year:

FEMALE DEPARTMENT, GRAMMAR SCHOOL NO. —,
New York, October 5, 1896.

Seating capacity of kitchen 35
Number of hours and minutes the teacher of cooking is employed each week in this department .... 2 hours 30 minutes

	Second grade.	Third grade.
Number of classes	1	1
Number in each class	19	29
Number receiving lesson in practice together a	5	5
Number receiving lesson in chemistry together	19	29
Length of each lesson in practice ....hours..	1½	1½
Length of each lesson in chemistry ....do....	1	1
Number of lessons in practice which each child receives per month a	2	2
Number of lessons in chemistry which each child receives per month	2	2
Total time given to instruction in this grade per month ....hours..	5	5

a Every child in each class is present at a practical lesson twice a month, but as only five can work at a time, each child has actual practice but two or three times in a term.

———, Principal.

FEMALE DEPARTMENT, GRAMMAR SCHOOL NO. —,

New York, October —, 1896.

Seating capacity of kitchen 45

Number of hours the teacher of cooking is employed each week in this department[1] 3

	Second grade.	Third grade.
Number of classes...	1	1
Number in each class..	37	46
Number receiving lesson in practice together....................................	37	46
Number receiving lesson in chemistry together..................................	37	46
Length of each lesson in practice *a*.......................................hours..	1	1
Length of each lesson in chemistry *a*..do....	½	½
Number of lessons in practice which each child receives per month	1	1
Number of lessons in chemistry which each child receives per month.............	4 or 5	4 or 5
Total time given to instruction in this grade per month.................hours..	12 or 15	12 or 15

a The lessons in practice and those in chemistry are frequently combined. While some articles are being cooked, a lesson in chemistry can be given.

—————, *Principal.*

The course in cookery was given during the school year 1897–98 in 22 schools to 127 classes, numbering 4,130 pupils. The number of pupils in each class ranged from 18 to 45. The supervisor states that—

Three other schools will be ready in September, and I trust the above number will be more than doubled during the coming winter. The schools in which you see small classes are mostly schools for boys and girls, the boys taking the shopwork and the girls cooking. A few of the principals of girls' schools have divided their classes. This ought to be done in every school, and we are hoping it soon will be, for it is impossible to have satisfactory results with large classes.

Before January 1, 1897, three hours per week were allowed with divided classes, so that the maximum number of pupils should never be more than 30. This division practically gave six hours to some classes though only three hours to each pupil. Afterwards the time was reduced to two hours as the result of a prolonged investigation into such work in the United States and abroad.

In January, 1898, the board of superintendents reviewed the matter, and unanimously reported in favor of reducing the time to one and a half hours per week. On January 18, 1899, the school board adopted the recommendation of the board of superintendents.

QUALIFICATIONS OF TEACHERS.

The board of superintendents of Manhattan and the Bronx established the following qualifications for supervisors and teachers of cookery in the schools under their control:

SPECIAL TEACHERS OF COOKING.

(*a*) Must give evidence of good general education and culture, and must have graduated from a course of professional training of at least one year, or must have had two years' experience in teaching the subject.

[1] Miss ——— remains in school from 9 a. m. to 3 p. m. All time not spent in instruction is spent in preparation.

(*b*) Must be examined in (1) chemistry and physiology of foods; (2) cooking; (3) hygiene; and (4) methods of teaching the subject, especially as shown by a practical demonstration lesson in the kitchen.

SUPERVISORS.

(*a*) A candidate for election as supervisor of a special branch must be (1) a graduate of a high school or of an institution of equal or higher scholastic rank; (2) a graduate from a course of professional training of at least one year in the special branch that he is to supervise or teach; and (3) a teacher of that special branch with at least three years' successful experience.

(*b*) Candidates for this position must give evidence of marked ability in the branches which they are to supervise.

Since the consolidation in February, 1898, of the various communities lying in and about New York Harbor into the city of New York a new régime has been called for, as a result of a chapter on education in the charter of the city. There is now one central board and one city superintendent over all boroughs, under whose direction a board of examiners provides an eligible list for all appointments, and who does all licensing. This central board has already issued one circular to candidates notifying them of an examination to take place on a certain date at a certain place.

The cooking schools are now to be found only in the elementary and evening schools and in the normal college, although they are also included in the authorized course for high schools and training schools.

The boroughs of Manhattan and the Bronx are educationally united under one borough superintendent, John Jasper, who alone thus far has cooking schools in his manual-training course.

Under his direction the course in cookery for the sixth and seventh school years has been revised and is now as follows:

OUTLINE OF THE COURSE OF COOKERY IN THE NEW YORK CITY SCHOOLS.

What cooking means.—Cooking means the knowledge of Medea and Circe, and of Calypso, and of Helen, and of Rebekah, and of the Queen of Sheba. It means the knowledge of all herbs, and fruit, and balms, and spices, and of all that is healing and sweet in fields and groves and savory in meats; it means carefulness and inventiveness, and watchfulness, and willingness, and readiness of appliance; it means the economy of your great-grandmothers and the science of modern chemists; it means much tasting and no wasting; it means English thoroughness, and French art, and Arabian hospitality; it means, in fine, that you are to be perfectly and always, ladies (loaf givers); and, as you are to see imperatively that everybody has something pretty to put on, so you are to see, yet more imperatively, that everybody has something nice to eat.—RUSKIN.

AIR, FIRE, WATER.

a. Their relation to life.
b. Their relation to cookery.

AIR.—*a.* Why important to life.
    1. Oxygen, with experiment.
    2. Necessity of fresh air.
    4. Relation to combustion.

FIRE.—*a.* Combustion.
    1. Kinds of ....{Slow—Examples of. / Rapid—Examples of.
  b Principal uses of fire in the house.
    1. For warmth.
    2. For cooking purposes.
  c. Fuels.
    1. History.
    2. Varieties.

                                                      Woods ....{Hard. / Soft.

                 Vegetable........{Fuels not in general use.{Peat. / Pressed hay. / Peach pits. / Corncobs. / Corn. / Camels' dung.

  a. Solid ....{

                 Mineral ....{Lignite. / Bituminous. / Anthracite.

                 Manufactured ....{Charcoal. / Coke.

  b. Liquid and gaseous..{Petroleum. / Alcohol. / Gases...{Natural. / Manufactured.

Note.—The attention of the pupils should constantly be called to the importance of economy in the use of fuels and of having fine connections for all gas stoves.

Note.—Could gas be universally used for fuel one of the greatest drudgeries of housekeeping—making and taking care of coal fires—would be removed. Every school kitchen is furnished with a gas stove, but great care and watchfulness on the part of teachers is necessary in order that the little cooks may form the habit of using it economically.

WATER.—*a.* Its source.
    1. Evaporation and condensation.
    2. Soft water—rain.
    3. Hard water—having taken mineral matter from the earth.
          Difference between .....{Temporary hard water. / Permanent hard water.
                        Tests.
    4. Impurities in water.
Note.—Caution in use of water that stands in pipes.

CHEMISTRY OF CLEANING.

1. Personal cleanliness.
  a. Care of ....{Skin. / Hair. / Teeth. / Nails.
  b. Care of clothing.

Note.—Their importance to the health of the individual and of the public, and their power as a preventive to the spread of contagious diseases should be dwelt upon.

2. Household cleanliness.
  a. Valuable aids to ....{Ventilation. / Sunlight. / Disinfectants.

  b. Care of ....{Beds and bedding. / Floors, walls, ceilings. / Closets, traps. / Pantries. / Ice boxes. / Dish towels. / Dish cloths, etc.

Note.—The study of the composition of soap, ammonia, soda, potash, etc., utensils, stoves, and polishing reagents, to be taken up under above heading.

THE HUMAN BODY.

a. Elements composing it and where obtained.

FOOD.—*a.* Its functions ...... $\begin{cases}\text{Growth.}\\\text{Waste and repair.}\end{cases}$

b. Food principles.... $\begin{cases}\text{Water.}\\\text{Nutrients ....}\begin{cases}\text{Protein.}\\\text{Fats.}\\\text{Carbohydrates.}\\\text{Mineral matter.}\end{cases}\end{cases}$

POTATOES.

Theory.—**History.**
Botany—Note difference between sweet and white potatoes.
Composition.

Experiment showing .... $\begin{cases}\text{Water.}\\\text{Starch—test.}\\\text{Cellulose.}\end{cases}$
Use of microscope.

Drawing................ $\begin{cases}\text{Plant.}\\\text{Tuber.}\\\text{Starch grains.}\end{cases}$

DIGESTION OF STARCH.
a. Salivary glands.
b. Action of saliva on starch.
c. Test saliva with litmus.
d. Pancreatic juice.
e. Food value of starch.

Practice.—Boiled.
Baked. $\begin{cases}\text{White.}\\\text{Sweet.}\end{cases}$
Mashed.
Creamed.

Note.—Compare nutritive value of same.

CEREALS.
Theory.—History.
Botany—grow various grains.
Composition.
Note similarity and difference in grains.
Show cross sections under microscope.
Importance in the vegetable kingdom.
Prunes, figs, dates, bananas and other fruits, valuable adjuncts.

Practice.—Mush from various grains served hot and molded.
Note difference in quantity of water and time required in the cooking of whole grains and those in other forms.

Note.—Emphasize importance of having rice grains whole and dry.

BREADS.

Theory.—1. History of breads of various nations.
2. Materials used.
3. Made light by use of—
   1. Air.
   2. Gas—CO_2.... $\begin{cases}\text{From acid and alkali.}\\\text{From yeast fermentation.}\\\text{Aerated.}\end{cases}$
4. Baking powders.
   a. Their composition.
   b. Adulterations.
   c. Materials to illustrate.
      1. Cream of tartar.... $\begin{cases}\text{Argol.}\\\text{Crystal.}\\\text{Powder.}\end{cases}$
      2. Bicarbonate of soda.

Note.—Show other acids and alkalies. Tests. Experiments.

QUICK BREADS.

Practice.—Batters....{Thin—Example: Pop-overs, made light by air.
{Thick—Example: Muffins, made light by baking powder.

Note.—Make muffins of various kinds. *Quick oven necessary for all quick breads.*
Doughs—tea biscuit.
Short cake—using fruits in season.

YEAST.

Theory.—Botanical classification.
Manner of growth with experiments.
Use of microscope.
Drawings.
Fermentation....{Lactic.
{Acetic.

FLOUR.

Varieties of wheat and other grains used.
Milling processes.
Comparative value of white and whole wheat.
Separation of starch and gluten.
Use of microscope.

BREAD.

Processes in bread baking.
Temperature of oven in relation to size of loaf.

Digestibility....{Comparison between crust and crumb—
{Fresh and stale.
{Hot and cold.
{Toasted (properly).

Practice.—Whole wheat and white bread.
Bread sticks.

Rolls....{Parker House.
{Swedish.
{French.

OTHER WHEAT PREPARATIONS.

Theory.—Macaroni, spaghetti, etc.
Manufacture of.
Where most used.
Food value of.

Practice.—Macaroni with cheese.
Macaroni with cream sauce.
Spaghetti with tomatoes.

PROTEIN.

Theory.—1. Where found.
2. Its function in the body.
3. Varieties—chemical nature.
4. Digestion of:
    a. Under what conditions most easily digested.
    b. Mastication.
    c. Gastric and intestinal digestion.
    d. Experiments.

EGGS.

Theory.—1. Albumen.

   Note.—Above experiments under protein will cover most of the work
   with albumen.

2. Eggs of various birds: Those most commonly used as food.
3. Composition—Nutritive value.
4. Tests for fresh and stale.
5. Varying market value according to season.

28

Practice.—Soft cooked.
      Hard cooked.
      Poached.
      Omelettes .... { Plain.
                   { Spanish, etc.

TEA.

Theory.—History.
      Kinds.
      Properties.... { Stimulating.
                { Astringent.
                { Effect on digestion.
                { Test for tannin.
            Manners of preparing. Why?

COFFEE.

History.
Kinds.
Properties ... { Compare similarity and differences in tea and coffee.
              { Manners of preparing. Why?

COCOA AND CHOCOLATE.

Growth and preparation.
Nutritive value and digestibility.
Manner of cooking.

Note.—Practice work on beverages to be taken with bread lessons.

MILK.

Theory.—1. History: Milk of different animals.
        2. Composition, with experiments.
          a. Cream—Show globules under microscope.
          b. Amount of water.
          c. Casein.
        3. Nutritive value.
        4. Care of.... { Pasteurization.
                  { Sterilization.
                  { Cleanliness of utensils.

BUTTER.

Theory.—1. Dairy methods.
        2. Experiment.
          Make small amount.
        3. Flavors due to bacilli.
        4. Substitutes.
        5. Nutritive value.
        6. Digestibility compared with other fats.

CHEESE.

Theory.—1. Manufacture.
        2. Digestibility—Food value.
        3. Mold shown with microscope.

Practice.—Ramakins.
      Cheesed crackers.

VEGETABLE CLASSIFICATION.

Theory.—Seeds ..... { Peas.
               { Beans.

      Roots ..... { Carrots.
             { Turnips.

      Bulbs ...... Onions.

      Tubers .... { Potatoes.
            { Jerusalem artichokes.

      Shoots ..... Asparagus.

      Stalks .... { Celery.
            { Rhubarb.

Theory.—Leaves .... {Cabbage.
{Lettuce.

Flowers.... Cauliflower.

Fruit ..... {Cucumber.
{Tomato.

Fungi ...... Mushroom.

VEGETABLE PROTEIN.

Theory.—1. Where found.
2. Composition.
3. Large proportion of vegetable casein and corresponding difficulty of digestion if insufficiently cooked.
How to overcome this.

Soups.
Practice.—Purées... {Peas.
{Beans.
{Lentils.

Croutons.
Baked beans.

ANIMAL PROTEIN.

Theory.—1. Historical references.
2. Different cuts—their uses—comparative prices.
Meats—3. Food value and digestibility of different cuts, and effect of manner of cooking on same.
4. Methods of preserving.
5. Diseased meats—dangers resulting from their use.
Use of microscope showing fiber, bone, tissue, fat.
6. Care of before and after cooking.
7. Experiments with hot and cold water.

BROILING AND PAN-BROILING.

Practice.—1. Round steak—garnishing.
2. Chops.... {French.
{Loin—garnishing.
3. Meat cakes—garnishing.

ROASTING.

Theory.—1. Economy of flank or chuck.
2. Temperature of oven depending upon kind and size of cut
3. Necessity of saving drippings.

Practice.—Rolled flank, or chuck roast.

BROILING—SIMMERING.

Theory.—1. Difference in the broiling of fresh and salt meats.
2. Why flavor is not so good as in roasted meats.
3. Utilize water in which meat is cooked.

Practice.—Knuckle end of shoulder, or leg of mutton.

STEWING.

Theory.—1. Its relation to boiled meats.
2. The addition of vegetables.
3. Cheap cuts.... {Round of beef.
{Neck of mutton.
4. Slow cooking.

Practice.—Brown stew with dumplings.

BRAISING.

Theory.—1. Its relation to roasting.
2. Use of vegetables.
3. Cheap cuts and slow cooking.

Practice.—Liver. Under round of beef, larded, etc.

FRICASSÉEING.

Theory.—1. Materials used.

2. Kinds ....{White.
{Brown.

Practice.—Fowl, veal, etc.

FOWL.

Theory.—*a.* How to distinguish between young and old.
b. Preparation for market.
c. Purchasing of.
d. Game—
What it is.
Cost, etc.
Digestibility of.
e. Anatomy of.

Practice.—Fowl, roasted ....{Drawing.
{Singeing.
{Trussing.
{Stuffing.

FRYING.

Theory.—Different fats used.
Temperature necessary.
Difference between frying and sautéing.
Use of bread crumbs and egg.

Practice.—Breaded chops, tomato sauce.
Rice croquettes.

MADE-OVER DISHES.

Theory.—*a.* Economy of.
b. Care necessary.
Recooking hardens albumen, etc.
c. Materials used.

Practice.—Hashes.
Croquettes.
Minced meat on toast.
Rice and meat, etc.

SAUTÉING.

Theory.—*a.* Difference between sautéing and frying.
b. Food commonly sautéd.

Practice.—Liver and bacon—poor summer food.
Note difference in digestibility and nutritive value of internal organs
compared with other parts.

FISH.

Theory.—*a.* Kinds—Composition.
b. Native to what waters.
c. Light and dark, why difference in digestibility.
d. Fresh, salted, and smoked—Digestibility compared.
e. Nutritive value compared with meats.
f. How to tell fresh fish.

Practice.—Boiled.
Baked.
Broiled, sautéd, fried.
Garnishing.
Sauces.

31

SOUPS WITH STOCK.

Theory.—a. Stock—Composition.
        Little nutritive value.
    b. Manner of preparing, and why.
    c. Materials used.
        White of egg for clearing, and why used.

Practice.—Clear soups.
    Macaroni, noodles.
    Vegetable, tomato.
    Julienne.

    Note.—Use of scraps of beef, bones, etc.
        Use of water in which meat and vegetables have been cooked.

Soups without stock.

CREAM SOUPS.

Practice.—Potato.
    Celery.
    Mock bisque, etc.

Note.—Nutritive value.

BEEF TEA, JUICE, EXTRACT.

Theory.—a. When used; why used.
    b. Those only stimulating.
        Those both stimulating and nourishing.
    c. Methods of preparing.
    d. Cuts used.

Practice.—a. Beef tea.
    b. Beef juice.
    c. Combining beef juice with other foods.

VEGETABLES.

Theory.—a. Refer to classification.
    b. Use of vegetables in season.
    c. Importance of having them in fresh condition.
    d. Composition (general) and food value.
    e. Different methods of cooking.

Note.—A suitable vegetable to be cooked at each lesson on meats and fish. The history, composition, and adulteration of the condiments in common use will also form a part of the theory lessons on these subjects.

SALADS.

Theory.—a. Material used.
        1. Freshness and crispness of lettuce, etc.
        2. Left-overs of meat, fish, and vegetables.
    b. Value of oil used.

DRESSINGS.

Practice.—French.
    Mayonnaise.
    Boiled.
    Lettuce, tomato, cabbage, salmon, etc.

DESSERTS.

Theory.—a. Their relation to food and diet.
    b. Use and abuse.
    c. Use of fruits alone and in combination with other materials.
    d. Reason for the indigestibility of pastry.
    e. Use, composition, and adulteration of flavorings for desserts.

CUSTARDS.

Practice.—Soft, caramel, with sauce.
    Steamed, baked.
    Use of chocolate in.

SOUFFLÉS.

Practice.—Various kinds.
Use of dates, figs, and other fruits.

GELATINE JELLIES.

Beaten jellies.
Charlottes.

BATTER PUDDINGS.

Fruit used as variety.

CAKES.

Sponge.
Cup.
Molasses cake—cookies.
Layer cake.

SAUCES.

Suitable to combine with above desserts.

Note.—Study of the composition of different flavorings used in desserts, also adulterations of same, will form part of the theory lessons on this subject.

CANNING AND PRESERVING.

GERM THEORY.

Theory.—*a.* Foreign matter in the air.
b. Dust and what it contains.
c. Molds, yeast, and bacteria.
d. Show molds on bread, lemon, cheese, jellies, etc. Fermented canned fruits.
e. Souring of milk, soups, uncooked and cooked food, etc.
f. Use of microscope.
g. Food value of canned foods compared with other foods.

Practice.—Canning of fruits in season. Jellies, etc.
Comparison of modern methods of preserving with those of olden times.

FREEZING.

Theory.—*a.* Latent heat.
Principle of freezing.
Use of salt.
b. Packing.

Practice.—Ice cream.
Sherbets.
Frozen fruits.
Molded frozen desserts.

PHYSIOLOGY.

ALIMENTARY CANAL.

Theory.—*a.* Drawing, showing salivary glands, alimentary canal.
b. Saliva, gastric juice, pancreatic juice.
c. Experiments with saliva, pepsin, and pancreatin.

INVALID COOKERY.

Theory.—*a.* Necessity of a knowledge of.
b. How it differs from usual cooking.
c. Great carefulness and accuracy.
d. Daintiness—neatness.
e. Care in serving hot foods *hot.* Cold foods *cold.*

Practice.—Gruels—Beverages.
Beef juice, essence.
Egg preparations.
Milk preparations and combinations.
Oysters.
Jellies.
Ice cream.

INFANT FEEDING.

Theory and Practice.—Milk—care of, kinds.
Sterilization.
Pasteurization.
Care of bottles.

COOKING AND SERVING OF A SIMPLE DINNER.

Foods....{ Nutritious. / Economical.

TABLE SETTING—DECORATION.

Daintiness.
Spotless linen.

SERVING.

Quietness.
Carefulness, etc.

COURSES.

Soup.
Meat and vegetables.
Salad.
Dessert.

CONCLUSION.

Instruction will be given by the supervisor, at the regular conferences, on the division of the work of the different grades. The progress books kept by the teachers, showing the work covered each month, will be discussed and compared at these meetings.

In order to secure uniformity and mutual progress, each teacher will be required in turn to give a lecture on a subject chosen from the manual.

Free use of blackboard during each lesson is advised; also composition and dictation lessons for each grade.

Pupils should become familiar with quotations on cooking from the best authors, and with the names of the men in Europe and America who have made a study of this science. The pamphlets furnished by the Department of Agriculture in Washington will inform them of the investigations of food and nutrition made by the Government. Professor Atwater's Food and Diet is among these pamphlets, and should form one of the reading books in each class. Chas. D. Wood's Cooking of Meats is another such pamphlet.

Many valuable books of reference are to be found in the school libraries. Recommendations for others will be made from time to time in order to keep up with the progress in the investigations and research in this line of work.

Teachers will visit with the supervisor, from time to time, the manufactories of food products, such as flour mills, cream of tartar works, chocolate manufactories, canning establishments, and tea, coffee, and spice importing houses.

The following is a partial list of the reference books recommended by the supervisor for use in connection with the course in cookery:

Foods, by Edward Smith.
Chemistry of Cookery, by W. Matthieu Williams.
History of a Mouthful of Bread, by J. Macé, translated by Mrs. A. Gatty.
Remsen's Chemistry.
Laboratory Manual of General Chemistry, by Williams.
Vegetable World and Animal World, by Figuier.
Elements of Structural and Systematic Botany, by Campbell. (Boston, 1890.)
Principles of Hygiene, E. M. Hunt.

9900—No. 56——3

Spirit of Cookery (Thudichum).
Century Cook Book (Mary Ronald).
European and American Cuisine (Lemcke).
The Murrey Collection of Cook Books.
Francatelli's Modern Cook Book.
Marian Harland's Books.

The extracts given below from a letter by Mrs. Williams to the author of this report may serve to show with what earnestness and enthusiasm the work in cookery is being pursued in the New York schools:

Under the direction of the supervisor of cooking, teachers are expected to adapt from this general course such special courses for instruction as are suited to the peculiar needs of the environment from which their classes are drawn, thus combining utility with the pedagogical training given.

Cookery in the schools was for several years experimental, and was established in but few of our schools, but I am sure it was the hope of its advocates in the board of education that it would fill a long-felt want in the education of the girls in this great city. That this hope was shared by some of the principals of the pioneer schools whom it was my privilege to call friends I am equally sure.

It was not alone that the number of schools into which cookery has been introduced is greater than the entire number during the past ten years, but that it has also been extended to the first grades and college classes, and that we are so much better equipped to teach the work scientifically. * * *

Just as surely as the microscope and scientific research have accomplished wonders for the hospital, so will they accomplish wonders for the home. In order that the educational side of cookery might be better taught in our schools, in 1897 I asked for an appropriation of $214 for the purchase of microscopes. This amount was to supply each teacher with one, so that she could take it with her to different schools under her charge, and also to supply one powerful objective, which could serve for special work in all the schools. This application was readily granted, and I have since received an appropriation for twelve more microscopes. I believe the New York City public schools, borough of Manhattan and the Bronx, are the only schools in the country that can boast of the possession of these beautiful instruments for domestic-science classes. The use made of the microscope in the lessons on the chemistry of foods and of cookery, also of fire, air, and water, is shown in the work sent you. It is invaluable in our school. It develops the powers of observation, concentration, and judgment, and unfolds to the child the beauties of nature. There is much that can not be taught without it; for instance, the germ theory, fermentation in bread making, vinegar, cider, wine, etc. Decomposition, decay, disease, structure of fiber, trichina in fiber, composition of blood, are shown by its use in the meat lesson.

In the bread lesson the structure of and cell growth, structure of the grains, showing relative position and proportion of bran, gluten, and starch; in the lesson on water as food, purity of and cause of disease by drinking impure water, and in the lesson on milk, the necessity for sterilization, cheese molds and fungi.

A number of the pupils in one of the cooking classes of Grammar School No. 85 gave the lesson on the grains before the microscopical society a few weeks ago, and were highly praised for their intelligent work and beautiful drawings.

My teachers are working faithfully to keep up with the progress of all the sciences and research that bear upon the proper conduct of the home, and particularly the investigation relating to the food and nutrition of man. They have studied and worked with me in the biological laboratory of the New York University every Saturday during the winter, and we have planned to continue this study in connection with physiological chemistry at the summer course of this same university.

With such intelligent and earnest workers, do you think it too extravagant to hope that an article may some day be written telling that the teaching of cookery or home science has greatly reduced infant mortality, contagions diseases, intemperance (in eating and drinking), divorces, insanity, pauperism, competition of labor between the sexes, men's and women's clubs, etc.?

You have asked me my hope for the future for this work, and this is my firm hope: That this work, so truly woman's, will, by forming a part of every girl's education, bring about great changes in the home life. The girl who learns to-day the chemical composition of the potato, as well as how to cook it, will hardly, as the future mother, boast that her six months' boy "just loves" potatoes, nor will she be foolish enough to allow him a taste of everything at the table. She has been trained to know that the little white hearse has stood at the door of many a home because the young mother did not know how to feed and cloth and nurse her baby.

The "little woman" who has taken the lessons on combustion and economy in the use of fuels will not use the full force of gas in a half a dozen burners to cook her dinner, for she has learned that one burner turned very low will keep water at boiling point, and that no amount of heat can make it hotter.

The simple little experiments in the school kitchen on the composition of air have caused the little housekeeper to realize that it is positively injurious to health to sit in closed rooms on the winter evenings with lamps lighted or the gas stoves burning without any flue connections. And so it is with the lesson on the chemistry of cleaning. Our little girl is wonderfully interested in the bacteria of the dishcloth, and the ice box, and the garbage pail, and when she becomes mistress of a home these things will receive her attention as well as the parlor, library, and music room. If John can not afford to give her all these rooms, she has been trained to know that she can be just as happy if she must make one room answer the three purposes, and besides, being an American, she has this thought to comfort her, that under this glorious Government her thrift and economy may help to place her husband among the millionaires. With such a wife John will not need to go to the liquor store, nor will you see John, jr., among the boys who buy a hot fried cake for a penny and a cup of coffee for a penny, and stand in the snow and slush to eat them, as I have seen them do down in the Post-Office Square. For this little mother, I would have you know, learned how to make whole-wheat bread at school, and she knows that one of her nice light muffins and a little flat bottle of heated and cooled milk which she tucked in Johnny's pocket in the morning will give him more nourishment than a cart load of coffee and fried cakes. Such a little wife and mother is a blessing to her home and consequently to the State. If she has servants they are good ones, because she is a capable mistress. If she has not, she has learned to work so neatly and to so economize in time and strength that she scarcely misses them.

If the teaching of domestic science in our public schools produces such women—and it surely must—I think you will agree with me that the State and the nation reap the benefit.

The following statements have been taken from the printed report of the supervisor of cookery to the board of education, June 6, 1898:

Applications for the establishment of cooking classes have been made by the principals of (13 additional) public schools.

This is very gratifying when it is remembered that the number of applications made this year exceeds the entire number entered from the year 1887, when cookery was introduced, to the present year. These applications were obtained through the personal visits of the supervisor and were the voluntary acts of the principals. While this method of introducing the work consumed much time, it at least had the advantage of leaving no room for complaints, nor have any complaints been made; on the contrary, great praise and appreciation have been received from all. The supervisor earnestly recommends that the work be extended as rapidly as possible.

The cooking in the evening schools has been highly satisfactory, and it is greatly to be hoped that it may be introduced into evening schools for women during the coming year. The young girls and women who attend these schools are certainly ambitious for knowledge when they are willing to study two hours after a hard day's work. Great pride is taken in educating them for typewriters, stenographers, and bookkeepers, thus crowding the market with cheap labor. Would it not be better for the State if these women were taught just enough bookkeeping to enable them to keep the household accounts accurately and neatly, to understand taxation, to lease a house and know their legal responsibility as tenants, as they do in France? How many members of the class in chemistry in the Evening High School for Women have taken up that branch in order to better fit themselves to be home-keepers? Do they realize that there is no science so intimately connected with the very life of man as chemistry? How many would read with interest and profit the bulletins on the Chemistry and Economy of Food, furnished free by the Government? Probably not one. If, then, the study of cookery tends to fit our girls for their true station in life, and it is held by all who have made domestic economy their study that it does, should it not form a part of every girl's education?

EQUIPMENT OF KITCHENS.

All applications to the building and supply committees and departments have met with the most generous and courteous responses. An appropriation of $214 for the purchase of microscopes recommended by the supervisor was granted, and these beautiful instruments are the pride of the teachers of cookery and the principals interested in the sciences. At the request of the supply committee the supervisor was present when the awards for kitchen supplies were given out. She has also met the representatives of the building department at each new kitchen, in order to advise with them as to placing of blackboard, stoves, etc. Each kitchen is furnished with the following equipment:

Bath brick.
Whisk broom.
Brushes:
    Vegetable.
    Stove, blacking.
    Stove, polishing.
Oilcloth.
Cheese cloth.
Tablecloth.
Corkscrew.
Clotheshorse.
Napkins, fringed.
Stove polish, enameline.
Towel rack, roller.
Thermometers.
Bowls:
    1 qt., white.
    Large mixing, yellow.
Custard cups, yellow.
Cups and saucers.
Dish:
    Pressed glass, 8-in., plain.
    Vegetable, 8-in., oval.
Jars:
    Mason's 1-pt.
    Mason's 1-qt.
Jugs, 1-pt.

Nappies:
    8-in.
    7-in., scalloped.
Plates:
    Bread and butter.
    Dinner, 7-in.
    Soup, 6-in.
    Tea, 6-in.
Platters:
    Medium, 10-in.
    Large, 12-in.
Teapots.
Soup tureen.
Double agate boilers:
    1 qt.
    2 qts.
    4 qts.
Butter crock, 1 qt.
Carving set (knife, fork, and steel).
Cleaver, 7 in.
Soap dish, agate, hanging.
Forks:
    Table, plated.
    Kitchen.
Knives:
    Table, plated.
    Table, iron.

Knives—Continued.
  Bread.
  Chopping.
  Palette.
  Vegetable, French.
Larding needles.
Can openers.
Pans:
  Dripping.
  Frying, No. 1.
  Frying, No. 3.
Plates, agate.
Saucepan, lipped, agate, covered:
  No. 10.
  No. 14.
  No. 20.
Scales, large, with scoop, 12 lbs., No. 24.
Teaspoons, plated.
Tablespoons, plated.
Lemon squeezer.
Bins:
  Sugar, 5 lbs.
  Flour, 25 lbs.
Boxes:
  Bread.
  Pepper.
  Salt.
  Spice.
Apple corers.
Biscuit cutters.
Colanders, agate.
Egg whisk.
Flour dredgers.
Funnels, small mouth.
Graters.

Oyster broilers.
Potato mashers:
  Wire.
  Wooden.
Measures, graduated:
  ½ pt.
  1 qt.
Melon molds.
Pans:
  Bread.
  Cake.
  Dish, tin, one 4-qt.
  Muffin, iron, 8 holes.
  Muffin, 8 holes.
  Roll, 8 holes, Russia.
  Roll, French.
Vegetable, press (Hennis).
Coffeepots, 2 qts.
Shakers, soap.
Soup strainers, wire:
  Small.
  Medium.
Skimmers.
Sieves, flour.
Scoops.
Steamer.
Trays, japanned, oval, medium.
Tins, jelly-cake.
Dishcloth, wire.
Bread boards.
Chopping bowls, 12 in.
Dish mops, small.
Ice picks.
Rolling pins, revolving handles.
Spoon, wooden.

The furniture of the class room consists of a large marble-topped table (which serves as a dining table and as a demonstration table), kitchen table, dresser, specimen case, and clock. The floors are covered with linoleum. There are gas ranges, instantaneous water heaters, and large comfortable chairs with arm rests. Chemicals and chemical apparatus are purchased as required. In addition to the above a number of schools have the food charts published by the United States Department of Agriculture.

EXAMINATION OF APPLICANTS.

An examination of applicants for special teachers of cookery was held in October, 1897. Special subjects for the examination of candidates were suggested by the supervisor, and questions relating thereto were submitted by her. Six teachers were appointed from the eligible list.

VISITS TO SCHOOLS.

Visits have been regularly made, as shown in monthly reports, and such aid and suggestions given to the teachers as were found necessary. The city superintendent has been advised as to the appointments, transfers, and promotions of teachers.

CONFERENCES WITH TEACHERS.

Teachers have met the supervisor on Friday afternoon of each week at Public School 43, for lectures in chemistry. They were also enabled to do considerable laboratory work, as this school had been supplied with some chemicals and apparatus by the teacher of cookery (now supervisor) under an appropriation granted by the board of trustees in 1895. The lectures on the chemistry of food and of cookery were given by Mr. Sieberg, principal of this school, after 3 o'clock, through courtesy of the supervisor, who had been special teacher of cookery in his school for six years. These lectures, experiments, and the tests for adulterations in foods have proved invaluable to the teachers, and they feel that they have enjoyed an unusual advantage in this course. Mr. Hyatt, principal of Public School 85, is an enthusiast on cooking in the public schools, and he also has given valuable aid gratis in microscopy and botany to the supervisor and her teachers. As he has been a member of the microscopical society for thirty years, it was a great pleasure to study with him. And lastly, the teachers have met the supervisor every Saturday at the New York University, where she arranged for a course in biology with laboratory practice. The object of the course being to study the digestive processes of the lower animals, as a foundation for the study of the human alimentary system, special attention was given to those animals that serve as food for man.

The teachers have entered into the spirit of all this work with the greatest possible enthusiasm, and have given verbal and written expressions of their hearty appreciation of the aid and guidance of the supervisor. It has been a delight to her that her experience has made it possible to help them thus, and she thinks the board of education may be proud of this body of teachers who labor so faithfully to make themselves more able in their specialty.

COURSES OF STUDY.

A manual was prepared in October, 1897, by the supervisor and, by the direction of the special committee on instruction, was submitted to the secretary of the committee on manual training. After careful examination by him it was placed in the hands of the city superintendent, who duly examined it and, on November 30, decided to submit it to the committee on instruction with the recommendation that 1,500 copies be printed. Typewritten copies of this manual have been furnished the teachers until such time as it may be printed, and the supervisor earnestly recommends that it be done without further delay. The principals of the manual training schools are anxious to secure copies, and many requests have been received from various institutions throughout this country, and also from London and Canada.

The manual may seem perhaps to be too scientific for girls in our grammar schools, but we who teach from it are convinced that it is not. Many thousands of these girls never go beyond the grammar schools, and here or not at all they must be trained for the business they hope to follow through life, and this business is home making. Home making is the business of women by Divine right. In an age when all business processes are being put upon scientific bases, why should we not teach our girls that science bears an important relation to housekeeping in a variety of ways? The better they understand the philosophy of the ordinary things of life the better they will perform them and the easier it will be to fill their minds with a sense of the dignity of labor at home. The more they learn of the chemistry of cookery the fewer failures there will be. A girl should be taught the nutritive value of food as well as its cost; the sanitation of the home as well as its tidiness. Such training must produce prudent, economical, and thrifty housewives. They are much needed in America.

GENERAL REMARKS.

Many visitors from all parts of the country and from the various organizations and institutions in our city have been entertained by the supervisor, and all have expressed themselves as pleased with the manner in which this branch of manual training is being taught in the public schools.

Teachers have been gratified by the assurances of parents that the work was of practical value in their homes.

Numerous letters of inquiry and congratulation have been received and answered.

The library at the New York University has been placed at the disposal of the supervisor and teachers of cookery. All Government bulletins relating to food and nutrition have been furnished to the teachers at the request of the supervisor.

The schools in London and Paris were visited by the supervisor during the summer of 1897 and reports of visits given to the city superintendent and to the committee on instruction.

A resolution was passed by this committee, at the request of the supervisor, that the number in classes should not exceed 30. Most of the principals divided the classes exceeding that number.

Visits have been made by the supervisor and teachers of cookery to various food manufactories, flour mills, etc.; also to the aquarium and museum of Natural History.

The supervisor visited Pratt Institute, Philadelphia Cooking School, Teachers' College, and the food exhibit at Philadelphia for the benefit of her work.

This report will be closed with some examples of the lessons in cooking given by teachers in the New York schools during the past year, as well as of the work (written exercises and drawings) of pupils performed in connection with these lessons. This work was based upon subjects given to the teachers by the supervisor from the manual referred to before, and is a demonstration of the progress that has been made in a comparatively short time toward raising the dignity of home science by making the basis of the teaching the elementary principles of the science of food and nutrition and keeping the practical work of cooking in its proper place as a laboratory demonstration of the principles taught.

GIRL COOKING.
Drawn by E. A. C.

APPENDIX.

LESSONS, EXERCISES, AND DRAWINGS FROM THE COURSE IN COOKERY.

SYLLABUS OF LESSON ON WATER.

Experiments showing physical properties.

Boiling ..... { Use of thermometer. Testing temperatures. / Blood heat. Simmering. }

Evaporation. { Is it destroyed? / What is steam? Vapor? / Which is hotter? / Mineral matter remaining. / Why water assumes a spherical form when intensely heated. }

Solution .... { Some substances insoluble. / Starch. Sugar. Salt. / Boiling to recover the substance dissolved. }

Suspension.. { Chalk and insoluble material. }

Filtration... { Use of porous material. / A means of purification. }

Conclusions: The danger of it carrying disease-bearing germs or poisons in consequence of its great solvent power. Filtered to strain out or absorb visible impurity. Boiled to destroy invisible disease germs.

Chemical composition: Decomposition by means of the metal sodium attracting the oxygen of the water. Hydrogen remains. Tested for blue flame.

Impurities in water ..

Dissolves gases ...... { Showing why water should not be kept in contaminated air. / Boiled water is tasteless. Dissolved gases are lost. On exposing again to fresh air the gases, principally oxygen, will be reabsorbed. / Dissolves carbon dioxid, causing effervescence. / Fish will not live in boiled water. }

Dust may contain. { Organic or living matter. / Dead animal matter. }

Mineral matter. Lead. / Crust formed on kettle lids and in boilers. / Such waters better boiled before using. / Use of living matter in water.

Its influence on digestion: Digestion a softening and breaking up of food by means of body fluids. Indigestion often a want of fluid condition of digestive juices. Its wide distribution shows its importance, both to vegetable and animal kingdoms, and ranking it next to air in value.

Water as a means of cleansing: Different action of hard and soft water for this purpose. Hard water wastes soap. Importance of its liberal use.

Water for cooking purposes: The saving of food nutriment by use of the double boiler, where vegetables or cereals can be kept at a lower temperature for a longer

41

time than when boiled violently in direct contact with the fire.   Soups and boiled meats also better so cooked.

Vegetables and meats.
{
When put into hot water.
When put into cold water.
When put into salted water.
When put into fresh water.
}

H. P., Teacher.

PUPILS' EXERCISES ON LESSON ON WATER.

Water.—Water is a liquid formed by the chemical combination of the two gases, oxygen and hydrogen.   Water is capable of existing in three forms, as a liquid, a solid, or a gas.

When heated it goes off into the air as an invisible vapor, and when frozen it forms ice which is a solid.   When frozen it expands, a fact which is demonstrated by the bursting of pipes, a catastrophe which occurs frequently in winter.   When a solid is dissolved in water it is recoverable after the water has evaporated.   Hot is more capable of dissolving a solid than cold water.

Ninety per cent of fresh vegetables is water.   Three fourths of the earth's surface is water, and seven ninths of the human body is composed of it.   It is next in importance to air.

In burning sugar we discovered that it contained water the hydrogen of which burned with a blue flame.

Water used for drinking purposes should not be conveyed through leaden pipes because it absorbs poison from them.

As a classified food, water is a mineral or inorganic food, and its importance places it at the head of a long list of foods.   Water is so necessary to the body that a person can hardly live a day without it or some similar liquid.

E. E.

Water in cooking.—Soft water is best for cooking purposes, when the object is to soften hard vegetables or to make soup or stew of meat, and also to extract the flavor of tea and coffee.

Water is the greatest solvent.   But suppose we want to cook tender green vegetables or onions, if soft or rain water is used all the pretty green color and the flavor will be dissolved out.   So for these, use hard spring water or put salt in it to harden it.   We proved this by boiling one onion in salt or hard water and another in soft water.

The latter was all broken up and had no taste.   The first one was perfect in shape and had a delicious sweet flavor.   It had lost nothing.

———— ——.

Water.—Water is a compound it contains two elements oxygen and hydrogen. Hydrogen burns with a blue flame, this can be found out by burning sugar.

Water is a mineral and contains organic bodies.   It contains million of inhabitants they live on the organic matter or animal matter, they must be smaller than they are, these are called microbes.   If the water is an acid vegetable will appear in the water, if an alkali it will be an animal.   We can test this with litmus paper. The acid will turn red and the alkali changes back to blue.

Water does not dissolve all substances.   It takes one pint of water to dissolve two pounds of sugar and only six ounces of salt to one pint of water.   It also dissolves gases.   The purest water is rain, sometimes it is not pure, because there is sometimes a disease all over the city and when the first rain falls it collects all the impurities. The blood contains nearly 90 per cent water, vegetables 99 per cent, the body ⅞ per cent, an the earth three-fourths water.

We use water for cleaning purposes also for cooking.   Springs are produced by the rain first coming down and filtering through the porous material, that water contains a great deal of mineral matter, when water contains lime and magnesium it is very hard. Water is sometimes made hard by salt being put in it and allowing it to boil. Water absorbs the heat from the body. Fruits contain a great deal of water.

I. M.

SYLLABUS OF LESSON ON AIR.

I.

Ideas and facts to be developed during progress of illustrations and experiments.
- Air is first in importance of all that is necessary for life.
- Water ranks second.
- Solid food third.
- How air links our lives with that of plants.
- Most delicate of all substances (air thermometer the most perfect).
- Most powerful in motion.
- Without air we could neither see, hear, touch, taste, nor smell.
- The part it takes in cooking.

II.

Physical properties of.
- Invisible ......
- Inodorous .....
- Colorless ...... } Prove by observation.

- Elastic ....
- Has weight.... } Prove by experiment.

III.—CHEMICAL COMPOSITION.

Elements.............
- Oxygen the active element.
  - Experiment: to extract oxygen.
  - Two pupils assisting; class observing, making drawings of apparatus, and forming written conclusions.
- Nitrogen, diluting element.
  - Experiment: removing oxygen from a jar of air; making use of property of oxygen discovered in previous experiment.

Compound substances.
- Carbon dioxid, poisonous element: experiments to show how produced.
  - Respiration.
  - Combustion.
  - Decay.
  - Effervescence.
  - Fermentation.
- Moisture (variable); prove by experiments..
  - Combustion.
  - Respiration.
  - Decay.

IV.—DISCUSSION.

The discovery in 1894 by Professor Ramsay of another gas found in atmosphere and named *argon*.

V.—CONCLUSIONS.

(Placed by pupils on blackboard as they are formed.)

Oxygen ....
- Its history; when discovered; by whom; how widely distributed; one-fifth of air, proven; chief ingredient of water; in all organic matter; one-third of solid earth; one-half of minerals.
- Bathes the body internally, cleansing and removing all impurities by a slow combustion.
- Office of countless air cells in lungs.
- The gas that makes fires, all fuels, and lights burn.
- Result if air were undiluted oxygen.

Nitrogen ....
- Serves to render air less powerful.
- Nothing will burn in it; animals die in it.
- Puts out a flame instantly.
- Indifferent; neutral; does not easily combine.
- Found largely in firm animal tissues.
- Basis of animal bodies.
- Its wonderful activity when life ceases, combining immediately with hydrogen to form ammonia, a product of decay.

Carbon dioxid........
- The great source of plant nourishment.
- Interchange of elements between animals and plants.

	Takes in—	Produces—
Plant	Carbon dioxid	Starch.
	Water	Oxygen.
Animal	Starch and fat	Carbon dioxid.
	Oxygen	Water, fat.

VI.—CONCLUSIONS.

(With instructions for compositions.)

Importance of thorough ventilation.

Sufficient supply of pure air furnished.

Impure air removed—how make use of air currents.

A perfect nonconductor—air inclosed between two windows.

How temperature is measured—thermometer.

How weight is measured—barometer.

Simple experiments to prove pressure.

Air a mixture. Any one of its elements breathed alone would be dangerous.

How to best ventilate rooms.

Impure air the greatest source of sickness. We may have abundance of food and water, but if obliged to breathe impure air these blessings become a source of disease.

Importance of having with every morsel of food a corresponding morsel of air.

Sources of impurities must be removed. Teach others importance of doing this, and so remove the *cause* of disease.

Wholesome foods become poisons if our living rooms are not well ventilated.

Wrong to remain from one to two hours in ill-ventilated public buildings with numbers of human beings constantly poisoning the atmosphere.

Impure air the chief cause of consumption.

THE PART AIR TAKES IN COOKING.

Cooking of meats...
- The contained air in the tissues is expanded by heat, forcing the fibers apart, making more easily masticated. This is the point at which heat should be checked, as if further continued the material shrivels, losing flavor and nutriment with the moisture, and becoming dry and indigestible. This fact made use of in broiling and roasting.

Most delicious, light, and easily digested doughs are those made light by common air. Advantage of these over baking powder and yeast breads.

How moisture in air influences cooking.

How pressure in air influences cooking.

Cooking on mountain tops; in low valleys.

H. P., *Teacher.*

PUPILS' EXERCISES ON LESSON ON AIR.

Pressure of air.—Remove the shell from a hard-boiled egg and put the egg into the mouth of a wide bottle that will just fit it. You can leave it there all day and it would not move. The air in the bottle helps to press it up as much as the air on top is pressing it down and it is kept in the same place. If you were in a crowded place and people were pressing you on all sides alike you would remain in the same place.

Now take out the egg, and put a piece of burning match in the jar and let it burn out. Then quickly put back the egg and watch it slowly move downward and all at once drop into the bottle. The burning match expanded the air and it escaped. When the bottle cooled the air in it contracted and so filled a smaller place, as no more air could get in and there was an empty place between the air and egg and the force of air above the egg being greater, it was forced into the bottle.

E. B.

Nitrogen.—We had a pan filled with water and put a button fastened by a wire on the edge. Then we put a piece of phosphorus on the button and lit it, placing a bottle over the top. It made a very bright light, and of course anything burning must consume oxygen. We then saw a very peculiar thing happen. It was water going upward. This showed that an empty space had been formed in the bottle and something had to fill its place. Now, the water being nearest, it was used. This experiment also shows how much oxygen was used, and we found by measurement it was about one-fifth. This amount then showed the oxygen. We carefully lifted up the bottle, clapped over it a piece of glass. And now we test it as we did oxygen and carbon dioxid. A lighted match or taper was put out immediately. Animal life would be stilled in the same way.

F. E. C.

Gases of the air.—What is air? Pure air is an invisible fluid, made up of two gases—oxygen and nitrogen, without which we cannot live.

Men have been known to live without food many days, but man has never been known to exist without air.

Oxygen is far too lively a gas to live in, so kind nature has diluted it for us with another gas called nitrogen. If a person were put into a room filled with oxygen his face would first turn red, then his body would turn the same color, then his heart would beat very rapidly, and finally the arteries about this most important of all organs would burst.

Oxygen will burn everything it comes in contact with. This accounts for the burning up process which is always going on within our own bodies.

Oxygen can be extracted from the air by the use of electricity, but as this is not easy to work with in a schoolroom, we use manganese dioxid mixed with an equal quantity of chlorate of potash.

To extract the oxygen from these two substances, they are put together into a test tube to which is attached another tube. The latter is of very small circumference and has two or three crooks in it. Then place a large pan on the table filled one-third with water and put in it a block of wood about one inch thick. Then take an ordinary jar and fill it with water and place upside down so that the mouth of the jar is about halfway on the board. Then heat the tube in which the chemicals are and put the tube to which it is attached into the water right under the mouth of the jar. The water in the jar will then be seen to disappear gradually, and in its place will be the oxygen itself. To prove this, take a piece of wood and thrust it into the jar. It will take fire instantly and burn with a very bright flame.

To extract nitrogen from phosphorus is still more simply done. Attach a piece of wire to a button and on the button place a piece of phosphorus, being careful not to touch it with the fingers, as it will burn to the bone. The wire should be attached to the pan so that the button will be just above the water without touching it.

If you give the phosphorus long enough it will burn of itself, but if you are in a hurry put a match to it. It will throw sparks in every direction, so you must be very careful not to go too near it.

Place a jar over the phosphorus while it is burning. The jar will be seen to almost fill with a thick, gray smoke, but the bottom of the jar will be about one-fifth full of water. Light a match and throw it into this smoke, and it will go out instantly. The gas which has filled this jar is nitrogen.

Oxygen and nitrogen are the two gases of which the air is mainly composed, but the air also contains a third gas, which is carbon dioxid, and is the gas that we breathe out from the lungs.

L. E.

SYLLABUS OF LESSON ON FOOD—ITS CHEMISTRY.

I.—INTRODUCTION.

1. Food defined .... { Ignorance of its meaning. / Ignorance of relative value.

II.—DEVELOPMENT.

1. Chemistry applied to composition.
   - Food divisions
     - Organic ...... { Carbonaceous. / Nitrogenous.
     - Inorganic .... { Water. / Mineral salts.
   - Food combinations—Importance of mixed diet.

2. Chemistry applied to preparation.
   - Cooking
     - Processes .. { Convection. / Conduction. / Radiation.
     - Changes ... { Starch converted to sugar. / Sugar converted to caramel. / Effect upon albuminoids.
   - Ferments .... { Yeast raised breads. / Preservation of food.

3. Chemistry applied to digestion.
   - Salivary—conversion of starches to sugar.
   - Gastric—albuminoids to peptones.
   - Intestinal—fats—emulsions.

III.—CONCLUSION.

1. Chemistry a safeguard .. { Adulteration. / Improper cooking.
2. Chemistry a means to happiness. { Knowledge ennobling home labor. / Knowledge surest road to economy.

E. A. C., Teacher.

PUPIL'S EXERCISE ON LESSON ON FOOD—ITS CHEMISTRY.

We have learned in our cooking class that everything we eat is not food, because only what nourishes the body can be called food.

We have also learned of what substances our food is made up, and which are best for the building up of our bodies.

We have learned that we must not eat one kind of food, but to combine different foods so that all parts of our bodies may be properly nourished.

We now know what makes our muffins rise, and what changes take place, when they are put in the oven, and what makes our dough rise after yeast is put in it.

We enjoy cooking at home very much now that we know why we do certain things, and what our food is going to do for us after it is cooked.

It pleases my mother very much to see me cook at home what we have made in school.

M. C.

SYLLABUS OF LESSON ON CEREALS.

Order Gramineæ ... Principal kinds ..
- Wheat.
- Oats.
- Rice.
- Rye.
- Barley.
- Maize.

Production......... Seeds of certain grasses sown in autumn or growing in all but coldest climates.

Composition ....
- Water.
- Protein.
- Starch.
- Fat.
- Salts.
- Cellulose.
- Diastase.

Food value.......... Contain every element necessary for nutrition at small cost.

Preparation ....
- Thrashing.
- Winnowing.
- Hulling.
- Grinding.

Manner of cooking .. Softening of starch and cellulose by addition of water.

Causes of loss ......
- Fungi..
  - Blight.
  - Mildew.
  - Must.
- Insects.
  - Beetles.
  - Moths.
- Birds ..
  - Many feed on insects and seeds injurious to grain.
  - Bobolink exception, causing great loss to rice growers.

Other uses of grain.
- Feeding and fattening animals.
- Imitation coffee.
- Intoxicating liquors.

Uses of straw ......
- Food and litter for animals.
- Hats.
- Mats.
- Bedding.
- Thatching.
- Packing.

Chaff ....
- Beds.
- Packing.
- Adulteration.

Origin of name .....
- Ceres, goddess of corn.
- Cerealia feast held in Rome.

Wheat ....
- Native of ..... Lands around Mediterranean.
- Varieties ....
  - Color ....
    - Red.
    - White.
  - Time of sowing ..
    - Spring.
    - Winter.
  - Appearance......
    - Bearded.
    - Bald.
- Food value ... Easy of digestion; almost perfect food.

Wheat
- Uses
  - Bread.
  - Breakfast foods
    - Flakes.
    - Granules.
    - Germs, etc.
  - Pastes
    - Macaroni.
    - Spaghetti.
    - Vermicelli.
- History
  - Introduced into China 2700 B. C.
  - Used as vegetable in early Middle Ages in England.
  - America greatest wheat field of the world.

Oats
- Varieties
  - Black.
  - White.
- Uses
  - Breakfast foods
    - Hulled.
    - Steamed.
    - Rolled.
  - Thin cakes from meal.
  - Food for horses.
- Food value
  - Very nutritious if sufficiently cooked and hull removed.
- History
  - In cultivation before Christian era.
  - Grown in colder climates than wheat.
  - Wild oats used for hay in California.

Barley
- Native of......Central Asia.
- Uses
  - Barley water.
  - Fermented liquors.
  - Soups.
  - Bread.
- History
  - First of all grasses used for food.
  - Up to middle of seventeenth century principal breadstuff of England.

Rice
- Native of
  - India.
  - Northern Australia.
- Food value
  - Large quantity of starch.
  - Little protein and fat.
  - Easy of digestion—one hour.
- Uses
  - Vegetable.
  - Cakes.
  - Puddings.
  - Adulterate wheat flour.
  - Fatten poultry.
  - Saki by fermentation.
- History
  - Food of one-third population of world.
  - Asia and America two largest rice fields.
  - Requires much water during growth.

Rye
- Native of......Black and Caspian seas.
- Food value
  - Next to wheat.
  - Harder of digestion, caused by acetous fermentation.

Rye
- Uses
  - Bread { Russia. Germany.
  - Thin cakes. Sweden.
  - Substitute for coffee.
  - Whisky / Kvass } By fermentation.
- Grows on poorer soil and in colder clime than other cereals.

Corn
- Native of .... America.
- Distinguishing features .. { Largest and handsomest. Bearing two kinds of flowers.
- Varieties
  - White.
  - Yellow.
  - Sweet.
  - Pop.
- Food value
  - Nutritious.
  - Rich in oil.
  - Cheapest cereal.
- Uses
  - Breads.
  - To cheapen wheat bread by admixture.
  - Vegetable.
  - Fodder.
  - Fattening animals.
  - Distilling.
  - Sugar.
  - Oil.
  - Paper.
  - Fuel.
- History
  - In cultivation before discovery of America.
  - In 1847 potato famine increased its use in Ireland.
  - Supplanting millet in South Africa.
  - National bread of Mexico.
  - Tortillas.
  - Polenta in Italy.
- Practical value { As they contain all the nutrients, meats and more expensive foods can be used in smaller quantities where whole grain is used.
- Specimens { Grains on the straw and the different preparations. Plants grown in school.

N. N.

PUPIL'S EXERCISE ON LESSON ON CEREALS.

Oats.—Oats are classed among cereals, and belong to the grass family. Long ago, when people believed in gods and goddesses, they thought that there was a goddess of corn, whom they called Ceres, from which they derived the name of cereals. They believed that she had a daughter named Proserpina, who was once taken in a king's palace and had to go there for a few months in every year. Her mother, being very much grieved at hearing this, would let nothing grow while she was away. In the spring of every year, Proserpina returned, and again things began to grow, as before Proserpina's absence.

9900—No. 56——4

Oats go through much preparation before being cooked. First they are cut and thrashed, then hulled, then steamed, and last of all, crushed, the last process, half cooking them.

Before going through these processes, oats consist of straw, which is at the bottom, the ear at the top, the chaff, which is the outside of the oat, and the grain inside the chaff, containing the bran. When oats are being tied, we call it, "Binding the sheaves."

In hulling oats, we take off the hull, and in rolling oats, we put them between rollers, after being hulled. The hulled oats take ten hours to cook, and the rolled take about two hours.

Rice, oatmeal, hominy and farina are cereals. The Scotch, especially, are very fond of cereals, and the Chinese are fond of rice. For the reason that cereals are strengthening, when a horse is ready for hard work or to race, he is given oats. They contain proteid, which is called gluten, and helps to build up the system.

R. R.

SYLLABUS OF LESSON ON BREAD.

"Remember thy bread and bake it well, for he will not be kept well that eateth his bread as dough."

I.

Materials ....
- Picture of harvest field.
- Different grains grown in the class room to study botany of.
- Study of the action of enzyms in germination.
- Samples of the different milling products.
- Picture of old-fashioned mill.
- Microscope and slides to study cross section of grains.
- Gluten, wheat starch, iodin.
- Yeast cultures.
- Supplementary reading: Bulletins and charts issued by the United States Department of Agriculture, History of a Mouthful of Bread, by Jean Macé.

History ....
- The bread of the different people of the world.
- What portion uses wheat flour and eats light bread.
- Besides the grains the use of chestnuts, Iceland moss, barks of trees, roots of plants.

Processes in bread making.

Mixing ....
- Neatness and care in measuring materials.
- Necessity for lukewarm liquid.
- Consistency of batter for different kinds of bread.
- Proper handling of the spoon.

Kneading ....
- Reasons for.
- Different methods employed.
- Which simplest and least tiring.
- How to tell when sufficiently kneaded.
- Danger from diseased hands.
- Different machines used.

Raising ......
- Reasons for.
- Temperature required.
- Length of time depending on quantity of yeast.
- Effect of too long raising.
- Necessity of covering the dough.

Baking ....
- Size of loaf and molding.
- Small loaves better—why.
- Temperature of oven.
- Effect of too hot or too cool an oven.
- Length of time for baking.
- Effect of heat in baking, cooking of starch—formation of dextrin in crust—killing yeast.
- Danger of underdone bread.

PLATE II.

BUNCH OF WHEAT.

Drawn by A. P.

II.

Flour.

- **Manufacture** —
  - Different grains used—which best, and why.
  - Visit to a mill.
  - Method of milling.
  - Different kinds of flour.
  - Test for good flour.
  - Which flour best for bread.
  - Why graham flour will not take the place of whole wheat.
  - Use of pastry flour.
  - Extravagance of using prepared flour.
- **Chemistry** —
  - Experiment to separate gluten from starch.
  - Test for starch.
  - Burning flour, to show presence of water and mineral matter.

Yeast.

- **History** —
  - Story of its discovery.
  - Visit to a brewery.
- **Biology** —
  - Study of different cultures under the microscope.
  - Its appearance—growth and comparison with other plants.
- **Chemistry** —
  - Action in bread making.
  - Experiments—growth in ice water, boiling, and lukewarm water.
  - Alcoholic fermentation—experiments—collect and test CO_2—distill for alcohol.
  - Acetous formation—souring of dough.
- **Uses** —
  - Leaven.
  - Bread making.
  - Fermenting liquors.
- **Stale yeast** — Cause of—bacteria present.

III.

Physiology —

- **Digestibility** —
  - Crust and crumb—experiments to show presence of dextrin.
  - Toasted bread.
  - Fresh and stale bread.
  - Slack baked—experiments using crumb of underdone bread to raise dough.
  - Sour bread.
  - Heavy and compact bread.
  - Mastication—experiment with saliva.
- **Value as food** —
  - Muscle and bone forming—heat giving. (See charts and bulletins issued by United States Department of Agriculture.)
  - Comparative value of different kinds of bread.

Economy of —

- Homemade more wholesome and economical.
- Left-over bread and crumbs used for stuffing and simple deserts and digestible deserts, especially valuable for children.
- Stale-bread crumbs, for dipping croquettes, etc.

Practical value of science in the home.

- Never will use boiling water in mixing the batter for the dough.
- Will bake bread in small loaves to get more crust.
- Will never eat hot, fresh bread, underdone nor sour bread.
- Will make use of left-overs.
- Will know which kind of bread will give most nutriment to the body.

"Bread is the staff of life;
The honor of the husband,
And the pride of the wife."

E. B., *Teacher.*

PUPIL'S EXERCISE ON LESSON ON BREAD.

Bread.—Bread can be traced almost as far back, as the first man. In different parts of the world, the natives use the cereal, which is the most abundant in their country. It is but a small portion of the world, that enjoys the luxury of good wheat flour. We should therefore, be thankful to our forefathers; who first planted the wheat, and enlightened the process of " Bread Making." We should show our gratitude, by trying to enlighten it still more.

The people in the northern part of Sweeden, bake their bread twice a year, and when eaten is like a brick. In Lapland, oats and the inner bark of the pine tree, are ground, mixed, and made into large, flat cakes, cooked over a fire. In Iceland, the iceland-moss, is used, as we use flour. In some parts of the east, quite a quantity of buckwheat is used. In Italy chestnuts. Rice-bread is the chief food, of the Chinese.

The nourishment of bread, depends wholly upon its preparation. Bread should be light; heavy bread, is very difficult to digest. The more compact the bread, the more indigestible it is.

The smaller the loaves, the more crust, which is easier to digest. The large loaves, are not apt, to be thoroughly cooked in the center; the yeast plant has not been killed. When eaten, the yeast will go on growing, in our stomach, changing starch into sugar, the sugar into alcohol and gas, then the alcohol into vinegar, thus causing disorder in the stomach.

Bread should be thoroughly masticated, the starch, while being chewed, will be changed, by the action of the ptyalin, into sugar, sugar being the easier to digest.

Stale bread is preferable at all times, it will crumble easier, and the juices of the stomach can operate much better.

Bread that has become too stale, for table use, should not be thrown away, it can be used for many different purposes, it may be used for puddings, stuffings, toast and rolling croquettes.

"The Baker,"—in olden times, was respected in the community, and occupied a high position.   F. L.

Recipe for whole wheat bread.—1 pint lukewarm water; 1 teaspoonful salt; 1 or 3 cakes yeast; flour enough to make a batter.

Directions: Put water and salt into a large bowl add salt. Mix yeast with a little water and add. Stir in enough flour to make a drop batter. Beat until full of bubbles. Cover with clean towel. Stand in warm place until light. Now add flour enough to make a dough. Knead until smooth and elastic. Put into greased bowl cover and stand aside until two or three times its original size. Divide into small loaves mold to fit the pan. Cover stand aside. When light bake in a hot oven for 30 m. Good bread should have much crust and little crumb, and should not be too close-grained. If the bread be heavy it will be difficult to digest. The whole wheat bread is more nutritious because it contains more gluten which gives us muscle and phosphate of lime which builds up bones and teeth. Sour bread is indigestible.

We should not eat fresh bread because it is difficult to digest, nor bread that is sour as the acid is bad for the stomach.

We can save all stale pieces of bread and use them for pudding stuffing and also for rolling croquettes.   L. McF.

Experiments with yeast.—Put some yeast in pure molasses. No action.

Fill another glass with lukewarm water add one teaspoon of molasses and a small piece of yeast. Stand in a warm place.

Bubbles rise to the top, notice a smell of alcohol. The liquid is in a state of fermentation.

Put a little of this liquid on a slide glass and examine under the microscope. We find a great many cells, these are the yeast plants.

U. S. Dept. of Agn., Bul. 56, Office of Expt. Stations

PLATE III.

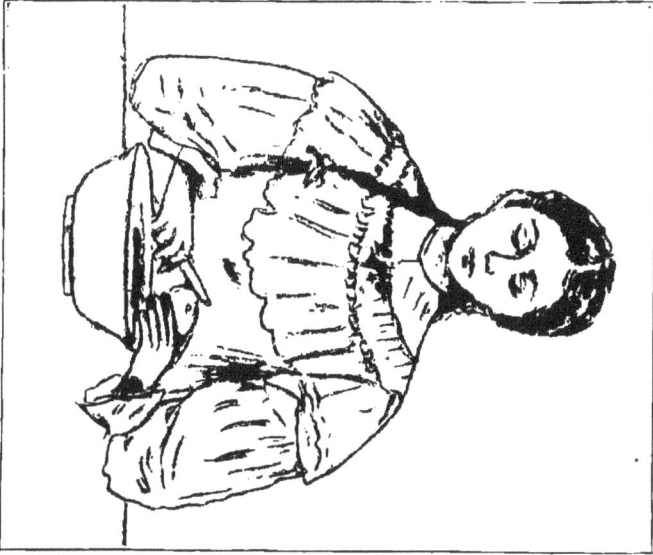

FIG. 1.—GIRL PARING POTATO.

Drawn by M. D., age 13 years.

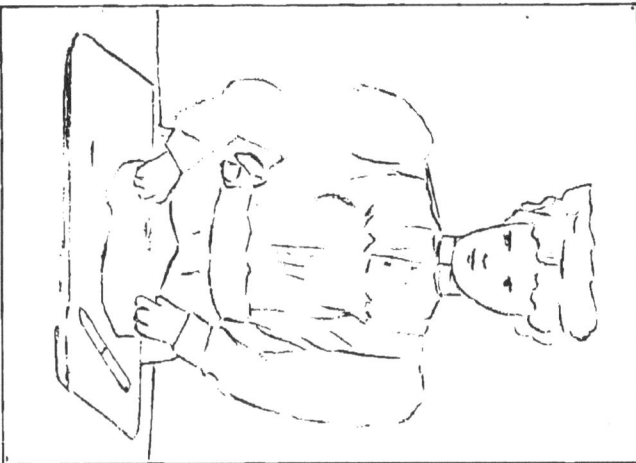

FIG. 2.—GIRL KNEADING BREAD.

Drawn by E. D.

U. S. Dept. of Agri., Bul. 56, Office of Expt. Stations.

PLATE IV.

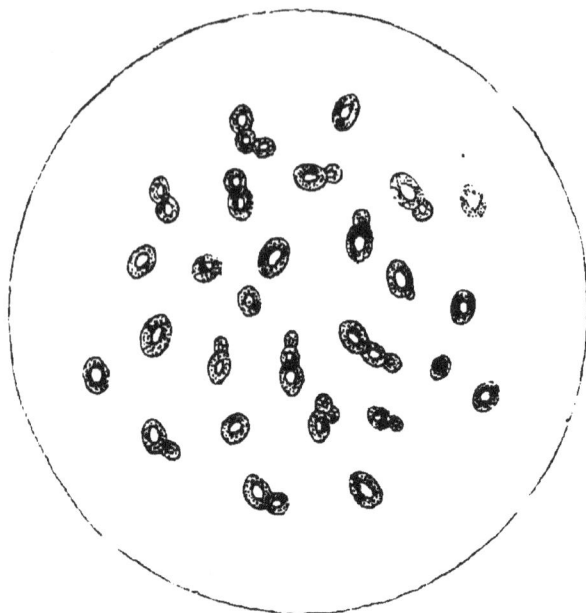

FIG. 1.—YEAST PLANTS AS SEEN UNDER THE MICROSCOPE.
Drawn by L. F.

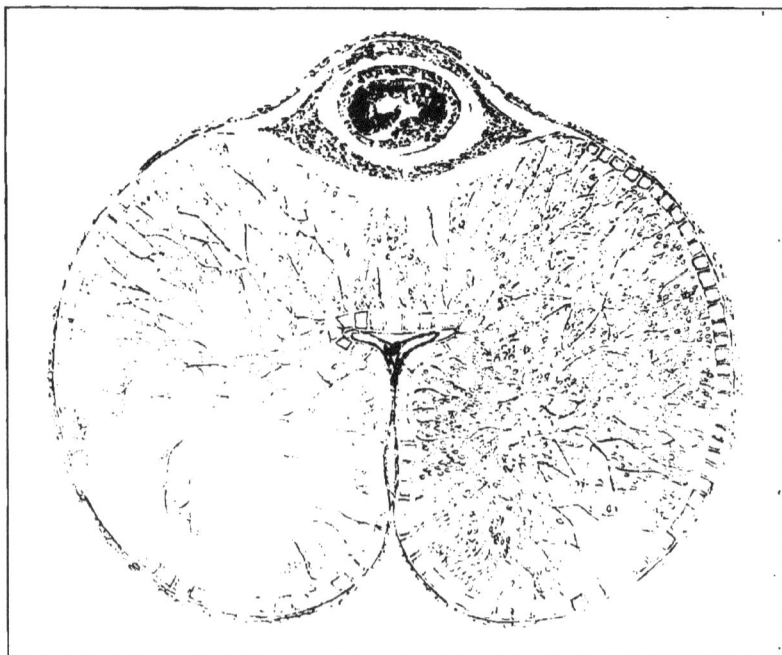

FIG. 2.—CROSS SECTION OF A GRAIN OF WHEAT AS SEEN UNDER THE MICROSCOPE.
Drawn by H. S

Some of them have sent out new cells like buds from them like other cells. Allow this liquid to stand for a day or so we get a strong odor of vinegar.

Mix yeast with ice water add flour as food and put it in the ice box.

Mix yeast with lukewarm water add flour as food and put it in a warm place.

Mix yeast with boiling water add flour as food and stand aside.

Examine these three glasses.

In the first no bubbles are seen.

In the second full of bubbles.

In the third no bubbles are seen.

This teaches us that cold water will keep the yeast plant from growing.

In warm water the yeast grows rapidly.

Boiling water will kill the yeast plant.

J. L.

SYLLABUS OF LESSON ON BAKING POWDER—QUICK BREADS.

Composition

1. Substances presented..{Cream tartar. Bicarbonate of soda.
2. Acids and alkalies discussed.{ a Vinegar, lemon juice, ammonia, soap, baking soda. b Tests with litmus.
3. Substances combined in definite proportions.
4. Small amount of starch used as a keeper.

Experiment

1. Effect when mixed dry—None.
2. Effect when moistened with cold water (H_2O).{Slight. Effervescence.
3. Effect when moistened with hot water (H_2O) ....{Greater effervescence. Violent escape of gas (CO_2).
4. Reason for not using liquid acids and alkalies—Too hasty escape of gas.

Practical application

1. Baking powder combined with dry ingredients.
2. Haste essential to prevent premature escape of gas ....{Moisture. Warmth of air.
3. Cooking.{ 1. Liquid in batter.}Gas formed. 2. Heat of oven....} 3. Muffins or biscuits rise. 4. Porosity of muffins or biscuits—Causes, spaces occupied by gas.

Test of purity.

1. Overabundance of starch—Thick when tested with boiling water.
2. Ammonia—Odor when heated.
3. Alum.{Solution made acid with $C_2H_4O_2$ (acetic acid). Decoction logwood added—purple color.

E. A. C. Teacher.

PUPIL'S EXERCISE ON LESSON ON QUICK BREADS.

Baking powder.—Baking powder is composed of two quantities of cream-of-tartar and one quantity of bi-carbonate of soda.

Bi-carbonate of soda is an alkali, and is sometimes made of common salt, but very often is obtained from a mineral substance called cryolite.

Cream-of-tartar is an acid, a substance dissolved in the grapes.

When the two substances are mixed there is no action between them. When a liquid is added there is a slight effervescence a small amount of carbon dioxid gas is formed. When they are moistened and heated a large amount of gas is formed.

When a mixture having baking powder in it is put into the oven, the carbon dioxid gas wants to escape and it carries the mixture up with it and the mixture becomes light and porous.

A. H.

SYLLABUS OF LESSON ON THE POTATO.

History ....
- Early ....
  - Native South America.
  - Spread into North America.
- Later .... Introduced into Europe.
  - By Spaniards, 16th century.
  - Ireland, Sir John Hawkins, 1565.
  - England, Sir Francis Drake, 1585.
  - England, Sir Walter Raleigh, 1586.

Botany ....
- Botanical name—*Solanum tuberosum.*
- Family—Deadly nightshade.
- Climate—Temperate.
- Part used as food—Tuber.
- Propagation—By buds or eyes.

Chemical analysis.
- Constituent parts ......
  - Water.
  - Starch.
  - Nitrogenous matter.
  - Mineral salts.
  - Cellulose.
- Experiment ....
  - Starch, water, and cellulose separated.
  - Starch test—Iodin.
  - Starch microscopically viewed.
    - Granules.
    - Cell walls.

Food value.
- Dependent upon cooking
  - Proper cooking of starch.
  - Softening of cellulose or vegetable fiber.
- Dependent upon dietary combination.
  - Fats.
  - Albuminoids.

Note ....
- Practical value of instruction.
  - Pupils will not serve waxy potatoes.
  - Will allow steam to escape.
  - Will not use potato water.
  - Will combine with food rich in nitrogen.
  - Will keep potatoes in dry, cool place.
  - Cook and thoroughly masticate all starchy foods.

1. McM. A., *Teacher.*

PUPIL'S EXERCISE ON LESSON ON THE POTATO.

The potato.—This vegetable is a native of South America, where it still grows wild. It was introduced into European countries by explorers.

The potato belongs to the same family of plants as tobacco. It contains a poison, peculiar to this class, which may be extracted from the potato by cooking.

The potato contains many compounds. The most important of these is starch. It also contains water, fat, cellulose, albumen and mineral matter. Starch is composed of carbon, hydrogen and oxygen. It is not flesh-forming but heat giving. A potato should be well chewed, so that the saliva can act upon the starch and change it to sugar. To cultivate the potato a good soil and a temperate climate are necessary.

Some think that the potato is a healthful vegetable. This is only so when eaten with food rich in nitrogen, for it lacks albumen. Served with eggs, meat, or fish, the potato helps to form a perfect diet.

The people of Ireland use the potato as one of the chief articles of diet. But they drink large quantities of buttermilk, or skimmed milk, which contains a great deal of flesh forming material.

The potato can be cooked in many ways. It can be baked, boiled, steamed, stewed, or fried. Of these the most digestible way of cooking is baking. A baked potato must be broken at one end, when taken from the oven, to allow the steam to

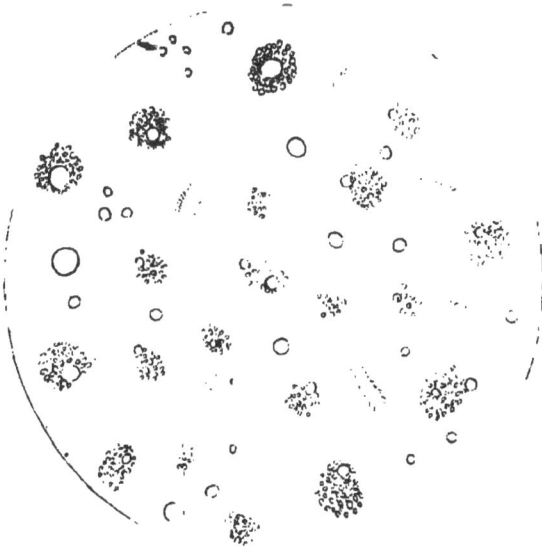

FIG. 1.—MILK AS IT APPEARS UNDER THE MICROSCOPE.

Drawn by M. P.

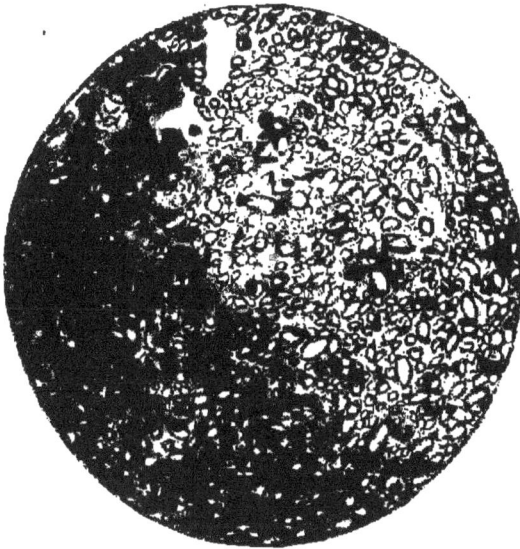

FIG. 2.—POTATO STARCH AS IT APPEARS UNDER THE MICROSCOPE.

Drawn by J. S., age 14 years.

escape. Boiled potatoes are also digestible; but the water in which they are boiled must not be used, because it contains the acrid juice. The potato when well cooked should be dry and mealy.

E. N., *Aged 15 years.*

The potato.—The potato is a native of South America, but was afterwards raised in North America. Sir John Hawkins introduced it into Ireland, where it is now the chief article of food, and Sir Francis Drake and Sir Walter Raleigh carried samples of potatoes from America to Europe. They first became popular as a food in the latter part of the eighteenth century. Before that time, they were cultivated in gardens and not in fields.

Potatoes belong to the nightshade order, a poisonous family of vegetables. They grow in temperate climates, and require a healthy soil. The part eaten is the tuber.

Starch, sugar, water, fat, cellulose, and nitrogenous matter are contained in a potato. Starch will not dissolve in cold water, only in warm water. When it is heated to $320°$, it changes to dextrin, or British gum.

When part of a potato is seen through a microscope the starch grains can be readily distinguished. When they are scarce, rice, or other starchy foods can be served instead.

Well-cooked potatoes should be dry and mealy; if they are waxy they are not digestible. Before serving baked potatoes, the skin should be broken, to enable the steam to escape.

R. S., *13 years, 3 months.*

SYLLABUS OF LESSON ON MILK.

Dairy industry......	Of great importance. United States considered one of leading dairy countries of the world. Chief occupation of great many farmers. Large quantities of products exported. United States does not consume as much as some other countries.
Consumers' knowledge of dairy products.	Where milk comes from, if clean farm and cattle healthy. If honest milkman, cause of dishonesty {Greater supply. Customers demand full measure at low prices.} Pure milk............{Not watered. Dirt or sediment. Diseased animals. Removal of cream. Preservatives.}
Fresh or sweet milk.	Rapid cooling after milking. How delivered from farms to supply large cities or country customers. Importance of care after delivered. Alkaline first drawn, neutral in about one hour. Acid in two or three. } Test with litmus. Appearance ....{Yellow-white. Mixture.} Composition ....{Water. Sugar. Fat. Casein, little albumen. Mineral matter.} Effect of standing...{Fat globules in suspension lighter than water, so rises to top of milk. Acid assists.}

Fresh or sweet milk — Milk called perfect food. Contains all substances to sustain body, not sufficient amount of some substances for adult.

- **Sterilized** — To kill germs or bacteria, keep from souring, heating to 212°. Should not be sterilized when used for babies or invalids. Casein hardened.

- **Pasteurized** — French chemist, Louis Pasteur. Heating to 160° kills germs without hardening casein and albumen.

Sour milk

- **Cause due to** — Organized ferments. Unorganized ferments.

- **Germs which are dangerous.** — From air. Unclean vessels. Diseased farm hands. Diseased animals.

- Apply to care in keeping milk and employing honest milkmen.

- **Parts of** — Cream. Curds. Whey.

Condensed milk — Removal of large amount of water by evaporation.

Butter made from cream or whole milk.

- **Process** — Churning in factories or individuals. Made from sweet or sour cream, usually sour. Fresh and salt.

- Rancid butter caused by presence of casein. Nitrogenous foods more favorable to bacteria.

- **Uses** — Used as addition to bread in cooking and an ointment in some countries.

- **Keeping** — Must be kept very clean and from all odors. Absorbs volatile odors very readily from cheese, meat, vegetables.

- **Adulterations** — Excess of salt covers odor and taste. Oleomargarine made from animal fat churned with milk. Butterine much the same as oleomargarine.

- **Tests** — Butter and oleomargarine heating.

Cheese

- **History** — Great many factories in the United States, England, Holland.

- **Kinds** — Whole milk.. Skim milk... Cream cheese — Great many different kinds come under these heads.

- **Coagulation** — Milk heated, then acid or rennet added. Separate curds from whey.

- **Process**
  - **Molding** — Pressed or shaped. Colored usually. Natural color pale yellow.
  - **Ripening** — Bacteria absolutely necessary in cheese to ripen it; not harmful; gives proper flavor as result.

Cheese .... {
Used as a food ...... { Highly nitrogenous. Very valuable. Muscle and bone forming.
Cooking.............. Renders more digestible.
Digestion .... Richer cheeses more easily digested.
}

A. B. H., *Teacher.*

PUPIL'S EXERCISE ON LESSON ON MILK.

Milk.—The dairy industry is carried on very extensively in the United States, but chiefly in the Middle Atlantic and North Central States. In large dairies where there are a great many men working, they should be careful to keep themselves and all the utensils very clean, as any dirt or harmful bacteria which may get into the milk are liable to cause disease.

Inspectors are appointed who go round and see that the farms, animals, and stables are thoroughly clean.

When milk is first drawn it is alkaline and warm. It should be put in a cool spring or where it will have fresh air and will cool quickly. Within an hour it becomes neutral and within a few hours begins to turn to an acid.

Dishonest milkmen often adulterate it with water. This for two reasons is harmful. The water might not be pure and the harmful bacteria might cause disease. Persons who are fed on milk do not get the amount of nourishment in proper proportions.

Milk is a perfect food for young children because it contains everything that the body needs: but for grown folks it is not; for this reason: although it contains most of the elements that the body needs yet they are not in sufficient quantities to sustain the life of a grown person.

When milk is to be transported milkmen sometimes put preservatives or substances into the milk (generally borax or soda) to keep it from souring.

Milk should be kept strictly cool, for hundreds of little bodies called germs which are floating around in the air some of which are friendly and others not, get into the milk and as they flourish in warmth, they grow and increase rapidly, sour the milk and are liable to cause disease.

Milk contains fat, water, sugar, mineral salts and casein but water is the most abundant.

The sugar of milk or lactose is sometimes extracted from the milk and sold at druggists for sweeting milk for babies.

Cream, which is the fat of milk being lighter than the other parts, rises to the top and is often sold separate. When the milk has stood for two or three hours the small amount of acid that is formed helps the cream to rise.

When the milk is boiled the casein hardens and so for babies it is not as nourishing as the unboiled milk.

A French chemist, Louis Pasteur, found that heating the milk to 165° kills the germs and leaves the casein soft. This preparation is called pasteurized milk.

If boiled or sterilized milk is left in an open vessel the harmful germs get into it again and begin their work. A good way to keep boiled milk is to put it in a bottle rinsed with boiling water so as to kill the germs the bottle should be corked with a piece of absorbent cotton. The air can get through this but the germs cannot.

Bottling milk is a much healthier and wiser way than distributing it from cans. The can must be opened at every customer's house and so the germs and dust get into the milk.

When germs get into the milk in the course of time they sour it.

When milk sours it separates into curds and whey, on account of the bacteria which have grown in it.

There are two kinds of ferments; the organized and the unorganized: the organized ferments are the germs and bacteria and the unorganized are rennet and pepsin; these will also separate into curds and whey.

The curds contain casein and mineral substances.

The whey contains sugar water and some of the mineral substances.

A great many things are made from milk. Butter is made by churning the cream, and the liquid which is left is called buttermilk. Cheese is made by heating the milk and adding rennet which separates it into curds and whey. It is then pressed so that the whey runs out, pressed again and shaped and has to stand for months so that the microbes inside it will have a chance to ripen it.   M. R.

SYLLABUS OF LESSON ON EGGS.

Production	Hen .... Duck .... Turkey .... Goose	Eggs of all birds edible. Fowls whose eggs are used for meat give greatest number of eggs. Negroes of Guinea consider eggs of boa constrictor an excellent article of food. Natives of Senegambia are fond of alligators' eggs.
Composition		Water—regulates temperature of body; helps carry off waste matters, etc. Albumen—muscle former. Oil—heat giver. Salts—bone maker.
Comparative weights of domestic fowls' eggs.		Hen, 1½ to 2 oz. Duck, 2 to 3 oz. Turkey, 3 to 4 oz. Goose, 4 to 6 oz.
Food value...........		Type of a nearly perfect food: more nutritious than twice their weight in beefsteak; yolk most nutritious part.
Cooking		Boiled. Baked. Fried. Omelets. Used in combination with other ingredients.
Other uses...........		Antidote in cases of poisoning by lead, arsenic, copper, mercury. Dressing for hair. Glue or mucilage. Tonic. In Russia oil separated from yolk and used medicinally. In Middle Ages yolk used for painters' art before discovery of oil colors.
Digestibility		Raw: Most easily digested form; not palatable. Added to milk, cocoa, beef tea, and many other foods, form an important part of invalid dietary. Digested in from 1½ to 2 hours. So-called boiled egg: Most agreeable form and very easily digested. Baked and fried: Very difficult of digestion; require from 3 to 4 hours. Omelets and scrambled eggs not so objectionable; due to mixture of white and yolk and to lightness.
Preservation	Keep from contact with air; evaporating water; desiccating.	Cover with some form of fat. Cover with limewater. (In both cases put small end downward and keep in cool, dark place.) Bury in earth. (Practiced by the Chinese with excellent results.)

Test of freshness ...... Put in bucket of water. Fresh ones will sink.

Commerce ....
{
In New York City amounts to 10 million dollars yearly.
In other cities proportionately large.
United States import 15 million dozen yearly.
}

Literature ....
{
Pope says: "The vulgar boil, the learned roast, an egg." (Satire VI.)
The Persians in a proverb: "If you be a cock, crow; if a hen, lay eggs."
Humpty Dumpty, etc., are well known.
}

Architecture .... Oval form the basis of many beautiful patterns in decoration and architecture.

Customs .... Hunting eggs at Easter a custom we have copied from the Dutch.

Points to be remembered.
{
Never cook in boiling water two minutes or more, as ordinarily done.
Give variety to the family by cooking the many kinds of omelets you have learned to prepare.
}
{
Point of coagulation, 130° F.
Proper point for cooking, 160° to 180°.
Hard and indigestible if cooked at 212°, boiling point of water.
}

Give only the freshest eggs to invalids.
{
Stale ones cause disorder of the stomach and cause a distaste for this most valuable food.
}

It is best to use lime-kept eggs or those not strictly fresh in the preparation of puddings, cakes, etc.

M. W. W., *Teacher.*

PUPIL'S EXERCISE ON LESSON ON EGGS.

Eggs.—The shape of an egg is considered one of the most beautiful as many fine architects use it for the base of columns by modifying it. Different kinds of eggs vary in shape a fowl whose flesh is eaten usually produces oval shape eggs and those of the sea fowl are pear shape.

The hen's egg is the smallest weighing one and a half to two ounces and ostrich egg is the largest weighing as much as three dozens of hen's eggs. The egg of the hen, duck goose and turkey are the kinds which are mostly used throughout the world.

In Africa the natives live chiefly on the egg of the ostrich and use the shells for drinking vessels.

All civilized and some barbarous nations use eggs as a form of food and consider them of more value than twice their weight in beefsteak. Raw eggs are the most easily digested and are an excellent food for invalids. In Russia the eggs or roe of the sturgeon are made into a dish called caviare which is considered a great luxury.

All eggs have two parts a white and a yolk, the white is composed of albumen, water and salt and the yolk is composed of albumen, water, salt and oil. Eggs contain everything necessary for animal life which is proved by the fact of a chick, a perfect animal, being hatched from an egg.

The well known custom of hunting for eggs at Easter was taken from the Dutch. One of Pope's saying's is "The vulgar boil, the learned roast, an egg." Many other legends are written about eggs. Humpty Dumpty being among them.

E. F.

SYLLABUS OF LESSON ON MEAT.

Materials ....
- Pictures of animals used as food.
- Cuts of meat.
- Drawings of sides of beef, mutton, lamb, veal, and pork.
- Microscope slides, showing fiber of meat in healthy and diseased condition; trichinæ in muscle.
- Picture of grazing cattle.

References ....
- Chemistry of Cookery, W. Matthieu Williams.
- Bulletins and charts issued by United States Department of Agriculture.

History ....
- Use of animals as food by ancients; what animals were used; how killed, prepared, etc.

Geography ....
- Where raised; importance of cleanliness and careful feeding; method of slaughtering and dressing; effect of refrigerating processes and improvements in transportation.

Effect of climate on kind of meat used.

Cooking
- Object ... — To render more sightly and palatable. To destroy bacteria and parasites.
- Principles
  - Boiling. Roasting. Broiling. Frying.. — Aim—to retain all juices in meat. Expose to great heat to coagulate albumen on surface. Smaller the piece, greater the heat.
  - Soups... Broth... Beef tea — Aim—to draw out all the juices. Soak in cold water. Draw out juices, but little if any of nutrients.
  - Stewing — Aim—to draw out part of juices and leave remainder in meat. Put into cold water, heat gradually to 180°.
- Method of rendering tough cuts tender.

Kinds of meat.....
- Animals from which obtained.
- Digestibility.

Cuts of meat......
- Their uses and cost.
- Nutritive value of cuts compared.
- Nutritive value as compared with cost.
- (See charts issued by United States Department of Agriculture.)

Care of meat ....Cooked and uncooked.

Tests of good meat .Color, texture, proportion of fat to muscular fiber.

Cost of meat ......
- Extravagance of constant use of steaks and chops; high price; amount of waste.
- Economy of using cheap cuts in form of stews and made dishes.

Left overs ....
- How to utilize; stews; hash; ragout; croquettes; meat balls.
- Nutritive value of.

Fats ....
- Rendering and clarifying.
- Importance of saving scraps.
- Necessity for using water to carry off impurities.
- Uses for frying, shortening, etc.
- Surplus to be made into soap.

Physiology ....
- How and where digested.
- Experiments; artificial digestion of different kinds of meat: beef, 1 hour; pork, 8 hours.
- Artificial digestion of fats with ox bile.

U. S. Dept. of Agri., Bul. 56, Office of Expt. Station.

PLATE VI.

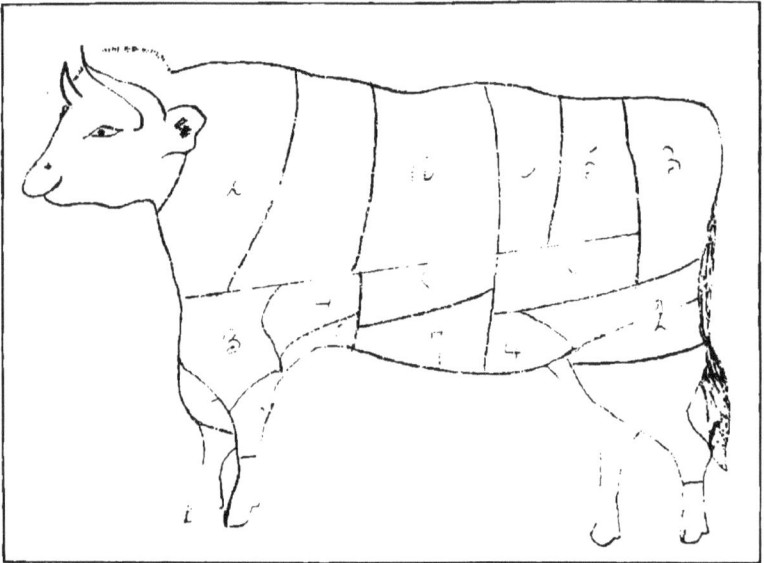

DIAGRAM OF CUTS OF BEEF.

1. Leg.	5. Porterhouse.	9. Top of sirloin.	13. Shoulder.
2. Round.	6. Sirloin.	10. Ribs.	14. Cross ribs.
3. Rump.	7. Navel.	11. Chuck.	15. Brisket.
4. Flank steak.	8. Plate.	12. Neck.	16. Shin.

Drawn by E. K., age 13 years.

U. S. Dept. of Agr. Bul. 56 Office of Expt. Stat.

PLATE VII.

FIG. 1. DIAGRAM OF CUTS OF BEEF.

Drawn by M. H., aged 14 years.

1. Leg.
2. Round.
3. Rump.

4. Flank.
5. Sirloin.

6. Porterhouse.
7. Flank.

8. Navel.
9. Plate.
10. Rib.

11. Chuck.
12. Shoulder.
13. Stew.
14. Neck.
15. Brisket.

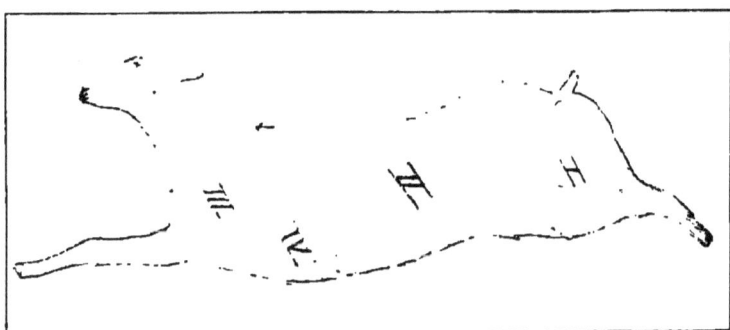

FIG. 2. DIAGRAM OF CUTS OF LAMB.

Drawn by A. O.

I. Leg.
II. Loin.

III. Shoulder.
IV. Breast.

V. Ribs.

III, IV, V together forequarters.

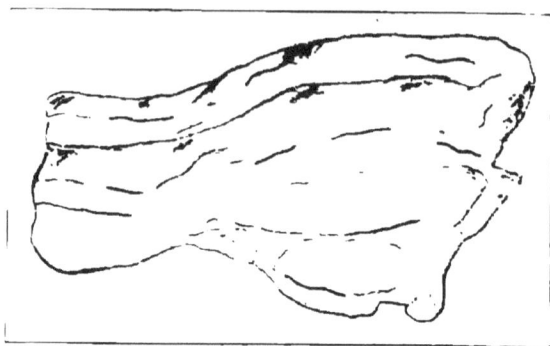

FIG. 1.—SMALL LOIN, OR PORTERHOUSE.
Drawn by E. W., age 15 years.

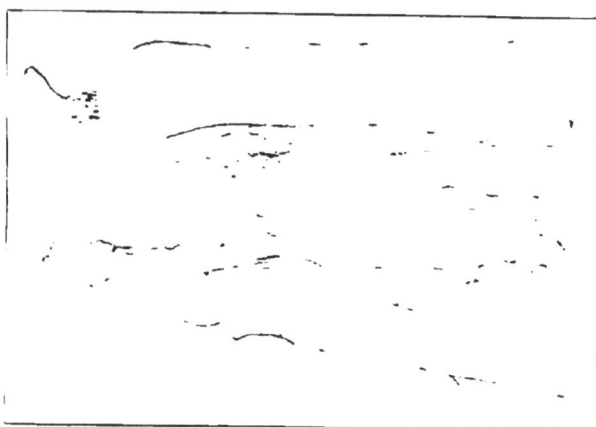

FIG. 2.—RUMP OF BEEF.
Drawn by J. D. E., age 13 years.

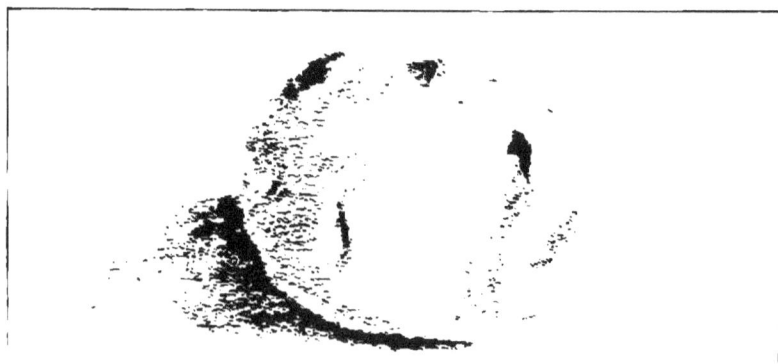

FIG. 3.—POTATO.
Drawn by M. P., age 14 years.

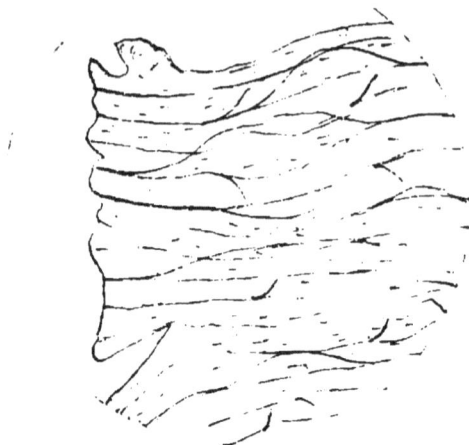

FIG. 1.—A PIECE OF BEEF AS SEEN UNDER THE MICROSCOPE.

Drawn by L. R., age 13 years.

FIG. 2. INDIVIDUAL BEEF FIBERS AS SEEN UNDER THE MICROSCOPE.

Drawn by L. R., age 13 years.

Methods of preserv-⎫ Corning, smoking, canning.
ing ....⎭

Structure...........Fibers shown under microscope.

Composition of....⎰ Water, fibrin, albumen, gelatine, fat, mineral matter.
⎱ Use in the body; muscle forming.

The science teaching will aid children in drawing conclusions which may readily be put into practice in their homes, preventing a waste of money and of valuable food material.

It leads them to see that true economy is dignified and that it means not only economy of money but also of material.

The following are some of the facts which are impressed upon the child:

Don't think that because a pound of sirloin costs twice as much as a pound of flank that it is twice as nourishing; it actually contains less nutritive matter.

Don't keep meat that is left over until it spoils; use it at once.

Don't eat much pork or any that is underdone.

Don't boil meat; let it simmer.

Don't think that because meat falls apart it is tender; connective tissue has been softened, but fibers toughened.

Don't fry in a small amount of fat.

Don't throw away the dish gravy; it should go into the soup kettle.

Don't put steak bones into the garbage pail; they will add flavor to a sauce or a soup.

M. I., Teacher.

PUPILS' EXERCISES ON LESSON ON MEAT.

Stewed meats.—The tougher cuts of meat, such as, the flank, the leg, the shoulder, and in fact all the meats found in the lower part of the animal, require long, slow cooking Although cheaper than the tenderer cuts they contain just as much nourishment, are of better flavor, and may be made palatable in the form of stews.

To stew meat, cut it into small pieces and trim the edges. Dredge with flour and brown in fat. Cover with boiling water or stock and move to the end of the stove where it will simmer, not boil.

Cooking meat in boiling water toughens the fibres, while if simmered, that is cooked at 180 degrees, the meat is rendered tender and digestible.

Meat which has been boiled, when touched with a fork, will fall apart and seem tender, but it is not so, it is because the membranes which have held the fibres together, have been softened; but the fibres have been made tough and indigestible.

Beef stew to serve eight persons.

	Cents.
2 pounds shoulder	.12
Potatoes	.03
Tomatoes	.02
Parsley. ⎱ Celery.. ⎰	.01
Pepper.. ⎱ Salt..... Onion... Flour ... ⎰	.01
Total cost	.19

E. L., Age 14.

Meat.—Meat is very nourishing. It is one of the principal foods, and is composed of fibren, myosin, water, albumen, fat, and mineral matter. Albumen, myosin, and fibren make flesh, and mineral matter makes bone.

Meat can be cooked in the following ways: Roasted, broiled, stewed, or made into broth. The ribs are used for roasting; either chuck, porterhouse, round, and surloin may be used for broiling; either chuck, flank, round, neck, shoulder, brisket, and plate are used for stew; soup meat comes from the leg; beef off the round is suitable for beef tea.

M. H.

Meat.—Meat is very wholesome if properly cooked, but many people cooked it at too high a temperature and not for a sufficient length of time; this is often the case in the stewing of meat. It is not always the **most expensive meat** that is the best. If you get a good flank steak which is a very cheap form, it will be as palatable as the most expensive cut.

Pork is very hard to digest, and is more likely to be infected than any other form of meat. Pork requires six hours for digestion, while beef but one hour; mutton about the same time as beef, lamb three to four hours, and veal about five hours.

K. C., *Age 14 years.*

Left overs.—Nobody need throw away any meat. If by chance there should be any meat left over from the day before, we can make hash, meat balls, croquettes, or potted meat.

Any of these would serve as meal and if cooked properly would make a delicious dish.

Just as good a stew, can be made with meat which is left over, as with fresh meat.

These dishes can be improved by adding vegetables, stale bread soaked or made into crumbs.

The nutritive value of potted meat or meat ball can be increased by the addition of a cream sauce.

In cooking meat the second time it is important not to cook it too long as it will become tough and very hard to digest.

P. R., *12 years.*

SYLLABUS OF LESSON ON BEVERAGES—TEA AND COFFEE.

Objects used in presenting the lesson.	A tea shrub budding—picture of the flower. Leaves of tea (green and black). Picture of the coffee tree showing the blossom and berries. Different coffee seeds, unroasted, partly roasted, fully roasted and ground.
Practical work	The making of tea and coffee by the girls: (1) Infusion .. } Contrast. (2) Decoction. } The proper preparation of these beverages.
Principal chemical composition.	Theine. Caffein. Tannic acid. Development of the volatile oils. Substances drawn out by— (1) Infusion. (2) Decoction.
Physiology	Effects of these substances— (1) Upon the nerves. (2) Upon digestion. Use of beverages to the body. Suitable beverages for children.
Preparation of tea for exportation.	Different kinds of tea. Quality shown by their names.

FIG. 1.—BRANCHES OF TEA AND COFFEE.

1. Tea (a) bud, (b) flower.　2. Coffee (a) flower, (b) berry.

Drawn by A. W., age 14 years.

FIG. 2.—CEREALS.

Drawn by T. D.

Preparation of coffee.. {
Milling.
Roasting.
Various kinds of coffee and how to distinguish them by their names.
}

J. B., Teacher.

PUPILS' EXERCISES ON LESSON ON TEA AND COFFEE.

Recipes.—The water must be freshly drawn and the minute it has boiled the tea and coffee should be infused.

Proportions for tea: 1 teaspoonful of tea to each cup of water. Allow the infusion to stand 3 minutes. The tea-pot should be heated before making the tea

Proportions for coffee: 1 tablespoonful of coffee to each cup of water allowing this infusion to stand from five to seven minutes. The ground coffee should be put into a muslin bag or strainer and the boiling water poured over. Never boil coffee, the fine flavor is dispelled by boiling a mucilage extracted at the same time, which tends to make it flat and weak. All coffee should be ground just before using.

Tea and coffee.—The only right way to prepare tea and coffee is by infusion, but they are often made by decoction, and when made in this way, they are injurious to our bodies. When these beverages are prepared by infusion, the boiling water is poured over the tea and coffee, and they only stand a few minutes. Decocted tea and coffee are made from boiling water, and boiled. This boiling draws out the tannin from the leaves of the tea, and the grounds of the coffee. Tea and coffee that are prepared by infusion have a nice pleasant taste, but when they are made by decoction, they have a bitter taste, and their pleasant odor and flavor are lost. All albumenous foods are hardened and made indigestible by drinking tea and coffee that has been boiled. Tea made by decoction causes more indigestion than coffee. These beverages are very useful to warm the body when it is cold and cool it when hot; the cooling takes place gradually. They also supply our bodies with the necessary liquid food. They contain stimulating and refreshing properties, but are not necessary beverages for young people, but a great benefit to older people when properly used. It is necessary to have a knowledge of their composition to know how to prepare them in the right way.

There is a substance in tea and coffee called an alkaloid which causes both these beverages to be stimulants. In tea this substance is called theine and in coffee caffeine. Both of these are stimulating properties of tea and coffee. They weaken the nerves and take away the natural desire for food. Too much tea or coffee weakens the general health and causes nervous diseases. There is also an acid called tannic acid in tea, and a volatile oil. This oil is produced in the drying of the leaves. It gives the tea its smell and flavor. Coffee also contains tannic acid, but not so much as tea. It contains an aromatic volatile oil. This oil gives coffee a flavor and smell and is produced in the roasting of the berries.

H. S., Age 13 years.

Tea and coffee.—Among the principal household beverages are tea and coffee. They should not however be used too frequently because they are not foods that repair the body although they supply it with some of the necessary liquid food. The only liquid necessary to life is water and milk for very young children.

They contain stimulating and refreshing qualities which in tea is called thiene and in coffee caffiene. These act on the nerves as stimulants. When any substance is called a stimulant it should be used with care for when our bodies are over-stimulated weakness in that part is caused and too much tea and coffee cause weak nerves. Both tea and coffee contain tannic acid and a volatile oil. This oil is produced in the drying of the tea leaves and the roasting of the coffee beans. In making tea or coffee it should never be boiled because that draws out the tannin. Infusion draws out the thiene, caffeine, and volatile oils making these beverages refreshing and not causing the indigestion of other foods.

Tea is a native of China and Japan but it is also grown in Ceylon and India. In one year there are four gatherings of the leaves. The first crop is the best. After the leaves have been picked they are dried, put in heated pans, dried, rolled, then dried again, and then packed in chests and sent to the different parts of the world. Green and black tea come from the same shrub, but the green tea is dried quickly and the black more slowly.

Coffee is the seed of an evergreen plant and is largely cultivated in Arabia, South America, and the West and East Indies. It is allowed to grow from eight to ten feet and bears a pretty white flower which is succeeded by a red berry the seeds of which are the coffee beans each berry containing two seeds. The berry is gathered, the outer covering is taken off first and then the parchment-like covering which covers the two seeds. These seeds are roasted in a cylinder-like pan which is turned over a clear though moderate fire. They are then ground and are ready for use. The Mocha berry is a smaller and rounder berry than any other. Java and East Indian are a pale yellow and coffee from Brazil has a bluish color.

A. W., Age 14 years.

Recipes.—The water should be freshly drawn and the minute it has boiled the tea and coffee infused.

Proportions for tea: 1 teaspoonful of tea to each cup of water. Allow the infusion to stand three minutes. The tea-pot should be heated before making the tea.

Proportions for coffee: 1 tablespoonful of coffee to each cup of water, allowing this to stand from five to seven minutes. The ground coffee should be put into a muslin bag or strainer and the boiling water poured over. Never boil coffee, the fine flavor is dispelled by boiling and a mucilage is extracted at the same time which tends to make it flat and weak. All coffee should be ground just before using.

SYLLABUS OF LESSON ON DIGESTION.

To a thorough understanding of the nutrition of the body, a knowledge of those processes by which the food becomes part of the blood is most necessary: a knowledge of the normal conditions and the causes and effects of abnormal states of the digestive organs.

This requires a clear conception of the anatomy and physiology of the entire tract, and of the effects of various food stuffs and other substances on its work, and the result of different bodily conditions.

In presenting this subject to the pupil we have endeavored to bring it in a tangible form to the comprehension through sight, by the use of manikin, specimens, and various experiments.

Salivary digestion:

    Anatomy of the mouth—

        Tongue: its use.

        Teeth: their necessity, need for care, the effect on digestion of their loss.

        Mucous membrane: texture, experiments to show effect of astringents, as tannin in tea and coffee.

        Saliva: structure of salivary glands:

            From what saliva is made.

            How it reaches the mouth.

            Test for alkalinity.

            Experiments showing its effect on cooked and raw starch.

            Effect of slight acids on its function, showing the cessation of salivary digestion in the stomach. This points out the need of thorough mastication of starchy foods.

Esophagus:

    Structure: action of muscles in swallowing.

    Membrane.

65

Gastric digestion:
Anatomy of stomach—
Situation. (Distention may impede heart action.)
Microscopical examination of lining.
Muscles; action.
Gastric juice; where made, action shown by experiments, interference of its
work shown by various substances (superacidity, etc.). (This teaches the
result of large quantities of vinegar, etc.). Effect of fatty acids produced in
frying, effect of ice water.
Causes of fermentation, of vomiting in infants.
Absorption of digested substances.
Intestinal digestion:
Anatomy; microscopical examination of lining.
Juices; where formed, chemical composition, their actions on foods, experiments.
Vermicular motion of tract explained by means of rubber tube.
Value of some indigestible material.
Causes of constipation; preventive and remedy.
Diarrhea; causes and remedy.
Comparative spaces for digestion of starches and albuminoids in the digestive tract.
Effects on the digestive action of various bodily conditions; nervousness, fatigue, etc.
Kinds of food indicated in some digestive disturbances.

E. H. C., *Teacher.*

PUPILS' EXERCISES ON LESSON ON DIGESTION.

Digestion.—The teeth are very important to the process of digestion, as we cannot
chew our food very well without them; we should be careful to keep them free from
particles of food, to do nothing that may crack the enamel, for the least break will
give the microbes a place in which to settle and cause the decay of the teeth. The
first set of teeth is called the milk teeth and the second set is called the permanent set.

The mouth is moistened by a fluid manufactured from the blood and flows from
little glands under the jaw and ears into the mouth; this is called saliva and is
alkaline, that is, it turns blue litmus red. It contains a substance called ptyalin
which digests the starch we eat.

In our last lesson we made some experiments in the digestion of starch and found
that saliva digested cooked starch and changed it into dextrin. A drop of iodin in
starch always turns blue; but after this experiment the iodin did not change color.
This shows us that it was no longer starch. This new substance, dextrin, is the
form into which starch must be digested to enter the blood.

We also tested the digestion of starch with a drop of acid and found that saliva
did not digest the starch when the acid was present; we then tried the same experiment with a little vinegar; again we found that the saliva did not digest the starch.
This shows that we should not eat any uncooked starch, and as acids interfere
with the digestion of starch, they should not be eaten with it, nor will it be digested
in the stomach which is acid.

C. G., *Age 13 years.*

Digestion.—When our food is masticated it passes down into the stomach through
the esophagus or food pipe, which opens and closes again as the food moves along.
By means of this wave-like motion the food passes along the entire digestive tract.

The stomach and intestines are situated in the abdomen. The food remains in the
stomach some time, where it is churned about and some of it digested; then it continues its course into the duodenum, the upper part of the small intestine.

In the stomach is a slightly acid juice, called gastric juice; this digests only nitrogenous foods.

We made some experiments to see how meat was acted upon by the gastric juice;
we made same artificial gastric juice by disolving pepsin in some water and adding

9900—No. 56——5

a drop of hydrochloric acid. Pepsin is the digestive part of gastric juice. We put a small piece of meat into this in a test tube and stood it in a glass of water, which we kept at the temperature of the stomach. At the end of our lesson the piece of meat was very much smaller, it was being gradually dissolved by the gastric juice.

With a larger amount of acid the meat dissolved much more slowly, showing us that large quantities of acid food, like vinegar, interfere with the work of the stomach. We found that alkali also hindered the work of digestion. The delicate membrane lining the stomach is very much irritated by fatty acids of fried foods. The duodenum is very obliging, for it finishes the digestion of the substances that were not completed in the mouth and stomach. Materials that are not digestible, like the woody fiber of vegetables, are passed along the intestines in a wave-like manner and removed from the body. We should have some indigestible matter to keep the movement, and prevent constipation. Drinking plenty of water helps in this.   B. L. L.

SYLLABUS OF LESSON ON FUEL AND COMBUSTION.

Exhibition of materials.	Coal............	Hard. / Soft.
	Wood............	Hard. / Soft.
	Charcoal.	
	Coke.	

Fuel, early history....
(1) Used by prehistoric man.
(2) Method of igniting.
(3) Kinds—formation.

Coal............
(1) Importance—influence upon commerce.
(2) Formation.
(3) Geology.
(4) Chemical changes of wood—composition of coal.
(5) Kinds—usage.
(6) Geography.

Charcoal............
(1) Origin—method of formation.
(2) Composition of wood—elements driven off by partial combustion of wood.
(3) Residue.
(4) Ancient and modern usage.

Gas............
(1) Formation.
(2) Two flames...... { Blue, used in cooking. / Yellow, used to illuminate.
(3) Experiments with Bunsen burner to show perfect and imperfect combustion.
(a) Flames supplied with oxygen through openings in lower part of burner; also by surrounding air—result, flame blue; perfect combustion.
(b) Openings in burner closed—result, flame yellow; imperfect combustion—incandescent carbon.
(4) Study of gas stove. (a) Advantages. (b) Economy in using.

Combustion............
(1) Chemistry.
(2) Study of coal stove.
(a) Drafts.
(b) Placing.
(c) Kindling point.
(d) Products of combustion.
(e) Cinders.
(f) Ashes.
(3) Oxygen............ (a) Proportion in air. (b) Effect upon earth if air all oxygen

FIG. 1.—APPARATUS FOR GENERATING OXYGEN.
Drawn by A. McC.

FIG. 2.—ARTICLES USED IN CLEANING.
Drawn by I. G.

| Experiment .... | { Watch spring heated to kindling point and burned in pure oxygen. |

NOTE.—The practical benefit to be derived from this lesson by the children is the making and care of a coal fire; a knowledge of the comparative value of fuels and economy in the use of them.

D. E. M., *Teacher.*

PUPIL'S EXERCISE ON LESSON ON FUEL AND COMBUSTION.

Fuel.—Fuel is material used to produce heat by combustion.

Fuel of some kind is used by man to render food more palatable and digestible.

The first fuel used was dry twigs and branches of trees.

Before people had matches they rubbed two pieces of hard wood together and lighted the twigs by the sparks.

Fuel originated from vegetable matter which grew upon the earth many ages ago in the form of trees. These trees fell to the earth and gradually sunk below the surface, they passed through chemical changes until they were reduced to an impure form of carbon called coal. Coal is found in the United States, Great Britain, France, Belgium and Germany.

In our homes we generally use anthracite or hard coal but if we do not feed it with plenty of oxygen, it will not burn. All carbon readily unites with the oxygen of the air.

The fire is hottest when a blue and white flame comes up, but some people think it is hottest when it is red but it soon becomes low as most of the gas is burned away.

We should not put on coal up to the lids only up to the top of fire-box or the iron will become warped. We should put coal on lightly and often.

Bituminous or soft coal is cheaper but it gives out a great deal of smoke this is free carbon. Soft coal is generally used on railroad cars. If you take notice when you are sitting near an open window you will see little pieces flying about.

Gas is obtained from coal. There are two flames yellow and blue. The blue flame is the one to cook on as it is better fed by oxygen. The yellow flame is used to illuminate as it contains incandescent carbon if we should cook on it the cooking utensils would become black from the carbon.

Experiment to show that all substances will unite with oxygen when heated to kindling point. We took a flask and put in it some potassium chlorate and manganese dioxid and heated them. The oxygen was driven off through a glass tube into a bottle of water. The gas crowded out the water; then we took a piece of steel and lighted some sulphur on the end of it and put it in the oxygen, the sulphur heated the steel up to its kindling point and it burned.

So we know if the air was all oxygen every thing in the world would be consumed.

Charcoal is wood burned without much air reaching it. It is an impure form of carbon. There was not enough oxygen to burn it.   A. F. H.

SYLLABUS OF LESSON ON CHEMISTRY OF CLEANING.

I.—HOUSEHOLD CLEANLINESS.

(a) What it means:

(1) Keeping all portions of the house, both *seen* and *unseen*, free from *visible* and *invisible* uncleanliness.

(a) Visible uncleanliness:

Dust and dirt of various kinds—grease and other spots on woodwork, metal, marble, fabrics, etc.

(a) Invisible uncleanliness:

That caused by invisible particles of living matter floating in the air, usually occurring in dark, damp recesses, as waste pipes, drains, water-closets, pipes from tubs, etc. Closets and dark cupboards.

II.—Dust and what it Contains.

(*a*) Tyndall's experiment. (An account of.)
(*b*) Matter in dust easily detected.
(*c*) Matter in dust *not* easily detected:
    (Use of microscope.) Showing moldy bread, cheese, lemon, etc. Flour and water exposed to air for several hours. Explanation of causes of these conditions. Explanation of causes of unpleasant odors sometimes coming from dark, damp places.

III.—Aids to Household Cleanliness.

(*a*) A desire to be clean.
(*b*) Plenty of fresh air and sunshine.
(*c*) Free use of soap and water.
(*d*) Ammonia, washing powders, washing soda, kerosene, polishing reagents.

IV.—Chemical Nature of Soap.

(*a*) Alkalis used. {What happens when they are allowed to unite. Illustrated by
(*b*) Fat used .... { the making of soap.

V.—How to use "Aids to Cleanliness."

(*a*) Sunlight—kills germs; prevents their growth.
(*b*) Air, its composition; oxygen, its use and importance.
(*c*) Soap and water for almost all cleansing purposes.
(*d*) Ammonia, soda, and potash more powerful cleansers. When, where, and how to use them.
(*e*) Polishing reagents:
    (1) Why metals become tarnished, rusted, etc.
        Copper + zinc = brass. Brass acted upon by oxygen of air forming an oxid.
        Silver acted upon by sulphur.
        Iron, in presence of moisture acted upon by oxygen of air = iron rust.
        Nickel not acted upon by oxygen.
    (2) Different preparations used to remove tarnish, rust, dirt. Explanation of their mechanical and chemical action upon metals.

VI.—Care of Dish Towels, Dish Cloths, etc.

(*a*) Necessity of thorough washing in warm water and soap after each using; rinsing in clear warm water; drying in air and sunlight.
Growth of germs very rapid on dishcloths unless treated in above manner.

VII.—Sweeping and Dusting.

(*a*) Best methods of obtaining desired results.
(*b*) We *sweep* and *dust* to *remove* the dirt, not to *stir it up* and let it *settle* in another place.

VIII.—Care of Sink, Garbage Pail, etc.

(*a*) Sink.
    Use of hot water and soda.
    Use of strainer.
    Explanation of trap and its careful treatment.
(*b*) Garbage pail.
    Careful and thorough washing and drying.
(*c*) Disposal of garbage.
    By means of experiments, explanations, and the use of the microscope the pupils'

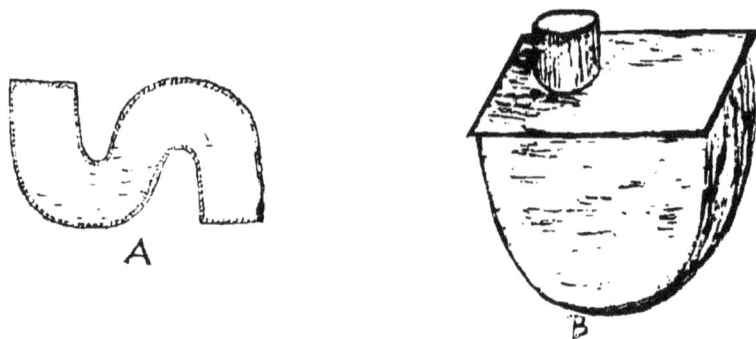

FIG. 1.—SEWER TRAPS: *A*, ∽ TRAP; *B*, ▭ TRAP.

Drawn by K. T.

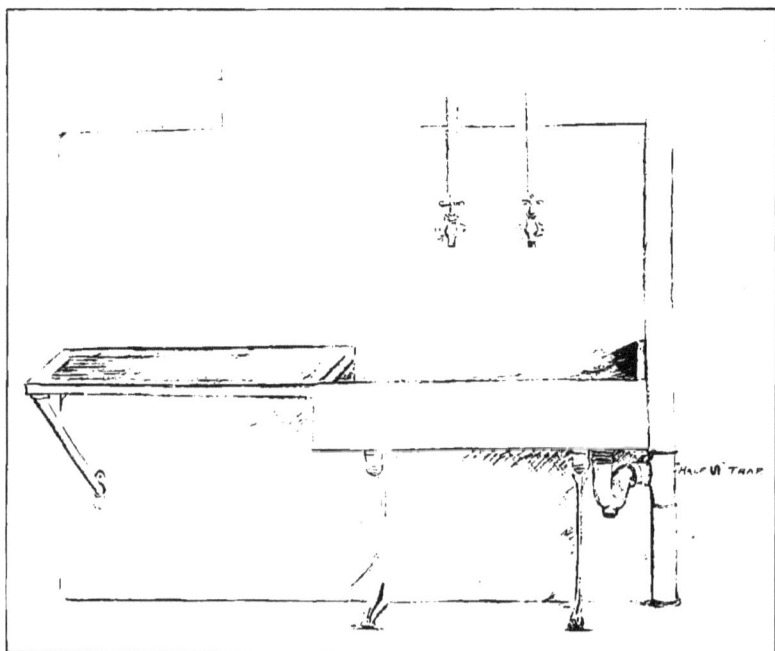

FIG. 2.—SINK, SHOWING "HALF-∽" TRAP.

Drawn by L. E. W.

69

minds are put in a questioning attitude, and daily more and more questions are asked. Most of the answers can be based upon scientific laws and principles, simply explained. These questions, relative to both cooking and cleaning, come not only from the pupils, but from the parents (through the children), showing that at home these matters are talked over.

C. G. J., *Teacher.*

PUPIL'S EXERCISE ON LESSON ON CHEMISTRY OF CLEANING.

The kitchen sink.—In olden times, sinks were not commonly known but, as the years have rolled on, changes came, and great improvements were made. Wooden sinks were first used, but they were very hard to keep clean, as the grease was liable to soak through the wood and cause bad odors. Now, iron sinks lined with porcelain, plain iron, and soapstone sinks are used. They are indeed very pleasing to the eye, and make kitchens look very clean and inviting, if kept neatly.

The faucets are fixed on the upper part of the sink, so that the water may flow down into the sink. They are made of brass or nickel and must be polished often.

A trap is a contrivance with a sort of bend in the pipe, which enables a small amount of water to be placed between the sewer and the dwelling; this preventing the entrance of sewer gases. There are different kinds of traps and the ones used on almost every sink in the city of New York are the ∽ or half ∽ traps (Pl. XII, fig. 1.1).

There are many other kinds of traps among the most important are the "◖," (Pl. XII, fig. *B*) "Bottle," "Round," and "Bag" traps.

Germs carried by sewer gas may cause most serious diseases, so upon the care of these traps largely depends the health of families. Unless the trap holds a certain amount of water, sufficient to form a seal to prevent gas from entering kitchens, it is of no value. Kitchen traps are difficult to keep clean and in good condition, as much grease is carried off by the dish water. When it enters the trap and waste pipe, it cools and clings to the sides. If a solution of washing soda and hot water is poured down the sink frequently, this can be prevented. Soda has the power of breaking the particles of fatty matter into very small parts, and then the hot water washes the matter away. A strainer should always be placed at the outlet and should be kept perfectly clean. I have seen careless servants scrape the leavings from plates into the sink, and try to wash little pieces of bones and sorts of food down the outlet. Perhaps illness has been caused by this uncleanliness. To be sure that this shall not happen, we must keep not only the trap of the kitchen sink clean and pure but all other traps as well.

K. T.

NOTES FROM THE CHILDREN'S EXERCISE BOOKS.

In looking over the notebooks of the children, also placed at the disposal of the author, it was found that the following facts were noted, which show clearly the basic principles of the instruction given:

C. S. says: "Starch is a heat-giving compound; * * it is a fine white powder composed of little granules. * * * Cold water has no effect upon starch granules, but boiling water bursts them. * * * When baking powder is put in flour, mixed, and moistened, the gas formed fills the flour with little bubbles, which form holes in the dough; when the mixture is put in the oven it hardens the dough about the little holes formed by the bubbles of gas, and the mixture is light and porous. * * * Yeast is the simplest form of plant life and consists of little cells which expand and grow very rapidly. * * * Like all plants, it requires heat and moisture; * * * it is called a ferment because it causes fermentation in dough."

J. G. says, in a lesson on the chemistry of food: "Food repairs the body by making flesh or muscle and by giving heat. * * * The heat or temperature of the body is about 98 degrees. * * * This heat is produced by combustion. One element alone will not nourish the body. * * * All food compounds are necessary.

* * * They are water, salt, mineral, fat, starch, sugar, and nitrogenous matter. ' * ' Albumen is a flesh-forming compound and is easily digested; it thickens by heat, fibrin by exposure to the air, casein by an acid."

F. S. speaks of the parts of an egg as follows: "Parts of the egg: Shell, membrane, white, yolk. Tests for fresh eggs: Light, water, shake. How to keep eggs fresh: Packed in closed boxes, sawdust, place in brine, limewater, cover with fat or varnish."

Albumen (Albus-white).

Effect on albumen of .... { Heat.
Acid .. { Citric (lemon).
Acetic (vinegar).
Muriatic or hydrochloric.
Alcohol.

C. L. says: "Food is that which is taken into the body to build up new material, to repair worn-out tissue, and to yield heat and energy. There are two classes of food—flesh formers, or nitrogenous, and heat givers, or carbonaceous. There are three classes of carbonaceous foods—fat, starch, sugar. Water is found in all foods. Mineral matter is found in all foods; helps to build up the bones."

A. K. says: "Cellulose is the woody fiber of the potato. * Cellulose forms the walls of the cells which holds the starch grains. ' * ' Cold water has no effect on starch. Hot water breaks the starch cells and renders them fit for food. Potatoes contain water, starch, cellulose, albumen, and potash salts."

S. T. gives the chemical composition of the potato as follows: Water, 75; starch, 18; fat, 0.3; mineral matter, 1; nitrogenous matter, 1; cellulose, 1; acid, 1; sugar, 2. She notes further: "How do we show that potatoes contain starch? By putting iodin in it; if it becomes blue, it contains starch. What other part did the experiment show us? It showed us the water and acid."

K. McG. says: "Skim-milk is as valuable as pure milk, only it differs in what it is composed of; it does not contain fat, but is nutritious if it does lack fat; it contains nitrogenous matter."

J. McW. says, in a note on starch: "After any food has commenced to boil reduce the temperature and allow it to simmer; we do this to avoid wasting fuel and prevent breaking of vegetable and also to prevent a hardening of albumen which many foods contain."

Among M. O.'s notes, it is stated that: "Food is that which is taken into the body to build up new tissue, to repair worn-out tissue, and to yield heat and energy."

In E. W.'s notes was found the following: "Rice contains more starch than any of the other grains; * ' * it is the most easily digested; * * * four-fifths of rice being starch, it should be eaten with some nitrogenous food, such as milk or eggs."

A. Q. says: "Is there starch in flour? We can find that there is starch in flour by putting a little into a glass with a little water, put in a drop of iodin, stir it, and when it turns blue we know it contains starch."

The above record with notes gives indubitable evidence of the fact that it is not simply cooking that the children are learning in these classes in the New York City public schools.

www.ingramcontent.com/pod-product-compliance
Lightning Source LLC
Chambersburg PA
CBHW021410090426
42742CB00009B/1095